Dr. Norman Sterrie

Three Blue Crosses

Edited by Al Zdon

Moonlit Eagle Productions
Minneapolis, Minnesota

Published by
Moonlit Eagle Productions
5064 Irondale Road
Mounds View, Minnesota 55112

Copyright © 2012 by Al Zdon

All rights reserved. No part of this book may be
reproduced or transmitted in any form or by any means, electronic or
mechanical, including photocopying, recording or by any
information storage or retrieval system without the written
permission of the Publisher, except where
permitted by law.
For information, address: Moonlit Eagle Productions.

ISBN: 978-0-9711940-3-8

Printed by Bang Printing, Brainerd, Minnesota
Manufactured in the United States of America

January, 2012

For all those whose life
is a service to others.

In our era, the road to holiness
necessarily passes
through the world of action.
-- Dag Hammarskjold

Acknowledgements

First of all, thanks to the Sterrie Family for their patience as this book was being prepared. A six-month project turned into a three-year project, but the family never wavered in its support. Cara Mearns-Thompson, the family's representative, was especially helpful.

Thanks to the Minnesota Historical Society and Doug Bekke for the use of an extended oral interview with Norm Sterrie done in 2007. About 95 percent of the book came from a series of taped interviews I had with Norm over a summer. But in Doug Bekke's excellent interview, Norm sometimes said things more clearly or more colorfully. Doug also had good copies of Norm's awards and certificates from World War II which are sprinkled throughout this book.

Thanks to all those who contributed pictures to the book. Bob Hall had photos of Norm's scrapbooks, and Bob Provost had photos of a World War II Round Table where I first saw Norm. Thanks to Don Patton of the Round Table who put me in touch with Norm. Norm's sister Eloise Cadman contributed some very crucial pictures to the book.

And thanks to the proofreaders Nan Williams and Larissa Zdon for their skilled attempt at making the book clean and grammatical. If there are any errors left in the book, they are mine.

-- Al Zdon

The first USS Lexington aircraft carrier.

PREFACE

I met Norm Sterrie sometime in the late 1990s when he was a panelist at a World War II Round Table meeting at the Ft. Snelling History Center in Minneapolis. I have always been a newspaper writer, and I was there to see if I could get a story for my newspaper.

Nearly all of those in the World War II generation have a good sense of humor, often dry and self-deprecating. It's a humor that was hard-earned -- growing up in the Depression and then coming to adulthood during wartime.

Dr. Norman Sterrie was one of the funniest guys I'd ever seen on such a panel. His humor seemed to be tinged with great wit and wisdom. His insight was both dead serious and wickedly funny at the same time.

Norm was introduced that night as having won three Navy Crosses, the second highest medal in the armed forces. I'd never heard of anyone before having three such awards. And I also heard that he was a pediatrician and that he played in the Minneapolis Police Band. I was intrigued with the breadth of his life, from war hero to baby doctor.

The next day, I called Norm and asked him if I could follow up on his remarks at the Round Table and do a story on his Navy career for the newspaper. He told me, basically, to hit the road. He didn't believe in glorifying war. I later found out that very few people at the large clinic where he worked (and which he ran for several years) knew anything in detail about his wartime exploits.

I had to use all my persuasive powers to convince Norm that my object was not to glorify war, but only to tell the story of the people who went through that time. He relented and he invited me over to lunch. Norm, whose wife Betsy had died a couple of years earlier, liked to make sandwiches. It was the first of many sandwich lunches with Norm through the years.

As time went on, I tried to convince Norm that a book would be a great way to capture his story for his family and for the rest of us. He wasn't very interested. Norm didn't affect modesty; he truly didn't believe in expounding on himself. As time went by, however, and Norm was asked to do more and more historical interviews, I think he began to have a notion that such a book might be useful.

Somewhere in 2007, he finally agreed. I went out and bought a new little tape recorder and showed up at Norm's house to begin our taping sessions. When I got there, he told me he had changed his mind. And that was that. I went home with my recorder still in its packaging.

In the meantime, I finished a book on Ken Dahlberg, another legendary flyer during World War II who had used his back pay from being in a POW camp to start what became the largest hearing aid company in America. When I showed up at Norm's apartment one day for a visit, he was holding a copy of the book on Ken. I think it gave him one more tangible reason to do his own. "Okay," he said. "Let's do it."

We taped every week throughout that summer of 2008. After I transcribed the 14 tapes, we went through them one by one. Those were my Fridays with Norm. I have to confess that there were many weeks that we ignored the book and just talked, and those were the best visits.

We were never able to actually come up with a title. We were talking about it one day, and I mentioned that the two torpedo bombers he flew during the war were the Devastator and the Avenger. "That's it," said Norm, with that wry smile. "We'll call it *Devastated and Avenged*."

As 2008 came to an end, one day Norm fell in the shower. His health had been fragile before that, but now breathing became difficult and his lungs were full of fluid. He died on New Year's Eve. He was 91.

Completing this book has been my way of keeping in touch with Norm. And as I go through the text editing and polishing, I can hear his voice, see the twinkle in his eye, enjoy his wit once more. I miss him a great deal.

Many thanks to all the people who helped with this book. Thanks to his family for their commitment to completing the project. Thanks to Norm for his friendship and for showing me how to get old with grace and dignity and humor. And thanks to Norm for his heroism in a war that truly saved the world from evil. And thanks to Norm for all the kids he helped through the years.

When God created man, it was people like Norm that He had in mind.

x

Contents

Chapter 1, **Growing up**, Page 3

Chapter 2, **Training**, Page 19

Chapter 3, **Going to War**, Page 27

Chapter 4, **Coral Sea**, Page 43

Chapter 5, **New Lexington**, Page 57

Chapter 6, **Philippine Sea**, Page 77

Chapter 7, **Homecoming**, Page 91

Chapter 8, **Music and Medicine**, Page 99

Dr. Norman Sterrie

Three Blue Crosses

Chapter One
Growing Up

Sogne Fjord is the largest in Norway, extending some 127 miles inland. Hafslo is a small village that these days has about 300 people. The famed Norwegian linguist Sylfest Lomheim was from Hafslo.

A website describes the region-having, "breathtaking fjords, steep mountains, abundant waterfalls, blue glaciers and luxuriant valleys." The region's main commerce is farming, growing berries and fruits, tourism and hydro power.

Norway and Emigration

My dad was the youngest of a number of children. They were raised on a farm in southern Norway near Hafslo. He was always proud of the fact that he was "Sogne," named for the area around the famous fjord.

My father, Ole Hess Sterrie, had a brother in Minnesota who had a department store in the southern part of the state. His brother's name was P.N. Sterrie, and he was the oldest in the family. In Norway, the oldest brother, of course, is entitled to inherit all the property and everything else in their system. Why he didn't stay on the farm is a mystery to me.

Being the youngest, my dad was kind of the leftover. He had been indentured out or at least left to help other people on their farms. I don't think that kind of life appealed to my dad. He emigrated at age 17 and joined his brother in the business, first in Elmore, Minnesota, and then later in St. James.

My mother, Ella Anderson, was a Carleton College graduate. How she got through school financially I don't know. She was a poor farm girl who had grown up near St. James. Before she got married, she had been teaching in northern Minnesota at Roseau, Bagley and Moose Lake.

My parents met in St. James and were married in 1915. I was born Nov. 14, 1917. I had two brothers and a sister, all younger than I. My parents always spoke English in the house -- unless they wanted to hide information from the kids.

I never envied my mom's life with dad because it seemed like we were always poor. We lived in a little two-bedroom house in St. James. There was no city water and no toilet facilities as we know them now. The heat was from a coal-burning stove. I shared a bed with my younger brother.

We had a big cow barn in the back of the house which was also a garage for our car, a Ford Model T. We would put it in the garage for the winter and not take it out again until the following spring.

My mother kept a flock of chickens in the back yard. We had to pick up the eggs every day.

Ella Anderson on the 1905 St. James High School Basketball Team.

Childhood

My mother never taught again after they were married – except me. She was a great educator for me. I suppose because I was the eldest son, she felt she had to put more time into it. I could read the funny papers at a very early age, and she taught me to read before I got to school. I remember one time when I was in the first grade, I had to read to the third graders. They plucked me out of class one day to read to the older kids.

I skipped second grade, and when I got to third grade, it was a rude awakening. I sat at the desk, and there was an ink well there. I didn't know what it was for because I'd never written with pen and ink.

Brothers Norman, Peter and Donald got a chance to hold some puppies.

There were probably 30 kids in a class. I only got into trouble once at the St. James School. I passed a note from one person to another, and the teacher intercepted it. I found myself in the superintendent's office getting 25 hours of extra time. I think the note had some profanity in it. It burned me that I was just the middle man. It wasn't fair.

I was in the Boy Scouts, and one of my projects was to write a history of the town. Mrs. Chapman was one of the ladies in my mother's Tuesday Club, and she lived a block off the railroad line on the north end of town. Her attic was full of old newspapers, and I remember going into that attic and digging out the history of the town from those papers. I don't know what happened to that history, but I doubt that it survived. I eventually became an Eagle Scout, the second one in our town.

Once, when I was a kid, I saw in a magazine one of those advertisements for chinchilla rabbits that would make me rich. I ordered a breeding pair of chinchillas. That expanded to about 25 rabbits that dad had to put up with buying hay for. There was no return whatsoever. I skinned one and decided that wasn't going to be my future. Ultimately, the wild dogs got into the pens and destroyed all of the rabbits, much to the relief of my father.

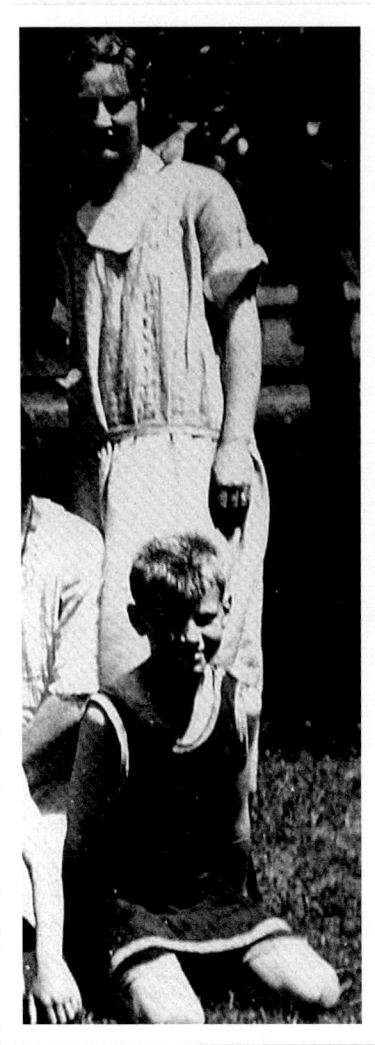

Norm and his mother, Ella.

My best friend was Clifford Curser who later became a teacher in the St. Peter School System. Besides typical kid's stuff, we played ball. We played field hockey with evaporated milk cans, and we did skating on the lake when they provided a rink for us out there.

Guns were a big part of early life. I remember having a rifle that I probably paid 50 cents for. It had been through many kids before me, of course. I also had a shotgun that cost about $2 and had also been through many friends before. Hunting was a great part of early life. I hid the guns out in the barn so mother would never know where we went on Saturdays, sneaking out the back way.

We would hunt pheasant sometimes — it was great pheasant country down there at the time. We shot ducks, and we loved to shoot at crows, but they were too smart. We never brought anything home, mother would have nothing to do with it. We'd sneak up on things by crawling on our belly through the cold and the dirt for a quarter mile or half mile.

The barn behind our house was a neighborhood gathering point for friends. It was a barn, a garage, a play pen. We used to play basketball out there if you can believe it.

St. James

The county newspaper was across the street from my dad's store. Upstairs of the newspaper was the Hammond Cigar factory. It was named after Minnesota Governor Hammond who grew up in St. James. There was a stairway in the middle of the building, and the kids could go up there and see a couple of guys making cigars.

I was working in the Sterrie Store one time when a customer came in and asked for a cigar. I reached in the box and handed him one, but he turned his nose up and wouldn't take it. I learned that you were supposed to hand the customer the open box and let him select it.

St. James was alive with celebration on "Ludefisk Day" in October, 1928.

The Penny's store was a few buildings down, and I remember that when you made a purchase, they put the money into a little basket and it would shoot up to the second floor where the cashier was. They had the same system down the street at the music store.

The Schmidt Bakery was nearby, and all the kids would go there for the candy. They'd press their noses up against the glass and pick out one of these and one of those. They'd get a nickel's worth of candy. The movie theater downtown was the Princess, and it was ten cents a movie. We'd always go on Saturday afternoon to watch the serials. They kept you hanging on the edge.

The first stop light St. James had was at the main intersection in town. There's a story about a guy named Gasink who had a team of horses. One day one of them dropped dead at the stop light. His comment was: "He never did that before."

The jewelry store was owned by Savert Hanson, and he also served on the school board. His son was the valedictorian the year I graduated. He later became a professor at St. Olaf. I wasn't smart enough to be the valedictorian, plus I had to work.

Near the railroad station was the F.M. Priest and Sons plant, and it did poultry processing. It was one of the major industries in town. A block to the north was a restaurant that opened very early in the morning. You could get coffee for five cents or eggs and toast for 20 cents. A lot of the farm wives came into that restaurant in the early morning, wearing their rubber boots, getting ready to

St. James, Minnesota, was founded in 1870, five years after the Civil War and during a time when the nation was expanding westward with great gusto. Railroads were being built all across the midwest. St. James was chosen as a site for a railroad center because it was midway between St. Paul and Sioux City, Iowa.

The story of the naming of the city involves Henry Sibley, one of Minnesota's most noted pioneers and business people. Sibley was a principal in the railroad, and he was offered the honor of naming the new city by the railroad's president, E.F. Drake. Sibley chose a fitting Indian name, but the next day, no one could remember it.

"Never mind, general, never mind," said Drake to Sibley. "We will have a name for the town we can think of. I propose we call it St. James."

By October, 1870, the rail line was completed through town, and buildings were going up.

St. James was the home of Winfield Scott Hammond, Minnesota's 18th governor, and also the home of Mike Kingery, who played Major League baseball. Not far from St. James, the notorious Younger Brothers were captured following the botched Jesse James bank robbery at Northfield.

work that day in the poultry plant.

St. James Lake was on the edge of town, and it was a typical southern Minnesota mud lake. After you went swimming, you'd have to look yourself over pretty good and take the leeches off.

We had a beautiful Methodist Church in St. James. The pastor for a time was the Rev. Mondale, and he had a son Buford who I knew pretty well. They later moved to Elmore, and Buford's little brother, Walter, later became vice president.

One year, about a week before Christmas, the church was full of kids practicing for the Christmas pageant. A candle got knocked over and started a fire, and the whole church burned down. That was one of the big fires in town. Another big fire I remember was at the grain elevator. I guess that's what grain elevators were famous for.

SCHOOL AND WORK

I had a great problem in junior high school and for a few years after with being in front of an audience. My mother tried to help me with that by signing me up in 4H, where we had to report our progress. She

Donald, Peter, Norm with Dad on an outing.

Norm is the hero, getting the fishing line down from the power lines.

stood by me and made me feel more comfortable talking in front of an audience. Unfortunately, I never wanted to take speech in college. I was afraid of it. But it would have been a tremendous help.

I graduated from St. James High School in 1934, and I was the honor student that year. I was not the top student in grades — I was down the list a ways, but The American Legion supplied a cup, a silver cup, to the selected boy or girl. You had to have excellence in studies, of course, and it said athletics on it, but not for me.

I didn't do any athletics in high school, it was all band. I tried out for track one time, but I fell down trying to do a hurdle. I picked the cinders out of my arm for the rest of my life. That was the end of my high school athletics.

The St. James Opera House, being restored in 2008, was also the home of the Sterrie Store, located on the ground floor, right hand side in this picture.

I had a girlfriend at St. James, and during my senior year it got a little too heated. We both said that was enough.

The new high school was built as I was growing up. I remember that a man was killed during the construction. He fell from the second story and was impaled on a steel rod. It shook up the community.

We were the first class to go all the way through the new high school. There was an alley behind the school that led to the Catholic school. Sometimes rock fights would break out between the "catlickers" and the "potlickers."

I was a junior in high school when I was hired by the Watonwan County Plain Dealer. It was a successful weekly newspaper. I was hired as a printer's devil. Part of the job called for me to set up an alarm clock at the newspaper every evening. When the alarm went off, the winder turned, releasing a weight that would turn on the Linotype so the lead would be melted by work time. If I failed, they couldn't get to work until the Linotype heated up, but I never failed.

Growing Up

The newspaper had one office girl out front. She was the typist, and she typed the whole newspaper before it went to the Linotype.

That was a wonderful place for me. Mostly I did everything in the print shop, set type, ran job machines, ran the big press and melted excess lead on Saturday mornings. I also learned to run the Linotype. I earned $20 for a 44-hour week.

My uncle and my dad's store was called the Sterrie Store, and it was general merchandise, agriculture, overalls. It was located on the ground floor of the Opera House. The farmers would come in every day with their eggs in these boxes, and we would have to count the eggs. I worked at the store as little as possible. I couldn't get the knack of wrapping packages, and that drove me out of the business. I didn't want any part of wrapping packages.

I also worked down the street at a gas station. You'd hand pump the gas up into this visible area that was marked so the customer knew how much gas he was getting. Of course, I also checked the tires, the oil and the rest.

My cousin had a truck route for delivering newspapers. You'd have to get up at four in the morning, catch the papers off the train, and deliver them to the smaller towns like Otten, Ormsby, Truman, Fairmont, and Sherburne. I had a regular route on Sunday mornings.

For companionship and sometimes for my safety, my dad would go with me on this route. I remember one blizzardy day, getting the newspaper bundles and not knowing whether we would make it or not, but we did. They had to have those Sunday papers you know.

All the money I earned I put in the bank. But the bank, Farmer's and Merchant's State Bank, went broke. In the end, they paid over 90 percent on a dollar, so I came out okay.

It seemed to me, growing up, that everybody in town was poor. The highest paid job in town was the superintendent of schools, and he was making $10,000 a year. My father somehow struggled through the

Eloise Cadman is Sterrie's little sister, the youngest of the family, and a graduate of Carlton College. She now lives in California.

"Norm idolized his mother. We grew up in hard times during the Depression. We lived in a simple house, and we didn't even have a washing machine. The Sterrie Store was a big store, and our uncle was a wealthy man. Our father worked for him. We never had much money, and it was mother who kept the household together.

Later on, my father had a different partner, but the store failed. Norm would go out with my dad and try to collect from the farmers, but they didn't have any money either.

Mother was a sensitive, gentle person and her ideals were extremely high. She worked very hard and she wanted all of us to succeed. She depended on Norm, and he was her helper.

We grew up feeling very secure. We had three aunts living very close to our home and cousins all over the place.

All the boys were involved with Scouting, and Norm earned the Eagle Scout award. He also had the cup from high school that said he was the outstanding student. That sat on our piano at home.

Norm was very good at playing musical instruments because he practiced so much. I remember one dance he played at that was in the hall above our store. I saw my parents dance, and I was so surprised. I'd never seen them dance before.

When Norman went away to war, I was very worried because I didn't like war. I prayed like crazy for him. All three of my mother's sons were pilots, and I prayed that none of them would get hurt because it would kill my mother. Norm was a very good letter writer, and we loved to read his letters. It meant that he was out there.

I had such pride in Norm, I was bursting with it. He was a knight in shining armor to me.

When he finally came home, they dismissed class so the whole school could go to the railroad station. And he was my big brother. It was so exciting. But when I saw him, it made me worry. He was a young man, but he looked so tired."

whole Depression, and we survived. Then he took on a partner – the man who was running the Penny's store. This fellow got into the money, and dad didn't find out until pretty late. He had to declare bankruptcy – it was the only way out of it. I was in my senior year at Carleton at the time in 1939, and I considered dropping out and going to work.

MUSIC

I played clarinet. I never took lessons. I just went down to the furniture store and picked out the prettiest instrument I could find. It cost $25. It was my first clarinet. Somebody gave me an old book of some kind that explained how to play it.

St. James had a downtown park, and as kids we would go down and listen to the band on Wednesday nights and Saturday nights. It was the St. James Fire Department Band. It was subsidized a little bit. They weren't very receptive to high school kids in the band because there was so much drinking going on.

After graduation, they were a little more receptive. Actually I played very well at that time, and I was useful as a band member.

I didn't dare tell my dad about the clarinet. He had

The Sterrie House in St. James in 2008.

Norman, Donald and Peter Sterrie with their sister, Eloise.

paid for me to have piano lessons at age eight, and I got tired of it. The teacher rapped me on the knuckles all the time with a ruler, and I couldn't take it. When I quit taking lessons, my dad said, "Those are the last music lessons you're going to have from me." It was 50 cents a throw. But I did learn how to read music.

I kept the clarinet in a closet downstairs, and the first time my dad knew that I played was when I played the solo in a band concert at the high school.

I had my own band in high school. As a senior, I had a trombone, trumpet, piano, and banjo in my band, and I played clarinet. I also bought a saxophone through a want ad in the Minneapolis paper. The fellow was willing to drive all the way to St. James from Minneapolis to sell that thing for $60 without any promise that he could even unload it. It was the depression years.

I bought it, learned to play it for my band, and it served me well. After the war I sold it back to Smith Music for the same $60. It was well worn. We were the Melody Masters, and we played popular music. For a 9 to 1 job, we were paid $12. One of the places we played was the "Bloody Bucket." There were a lot of fights there.

Later, I played in the Carleton Symphony Band. I was probably the only one in there who never had a lesson. I played among the first clarinets. The Carleton Symphony was a showpiece at the time. My sophomore year, they couldn't afford to support it any longer, but it had certainly been a concert band of note.

I also played in the college dance band. We got $100 a year for playing 12 dances. Of course it meant playing all the time while your lady friend was out there dancing with somebody else.

Just about three years ago, I had a stroke, and it took away the feeling in my right hand. With that went my music career.

Norm Sterrie during his time at Carleton

CARLETON

When I went to Carleton, I went with the idea I'd become a band instructor. I quickly learned at Carleton that I would never be able to achieve the level that was required to be a professional. Carleton had selected several students who had been the top students at Interlachen, the famous summer music camp in Michigan. I was in classes with those people. They were the top in the whole country. It was an eye-opener to the possibilities.

I had heard a lot about Carleton all my life, but paying for it was a challenge. I saved up $600 by working at the print shop, plus I had my little band. I gave Carleton that $600, and during the summers I could earn about $100 more. They accepted that as my tuition for the four years. To go to school for that price, I owe that school an awful lot.

While in college, I was hired by a small newspaper near Northfield. I would hitchhike up to that town, do about four hours on the Linotype, and then hop a freight back to Northfield. It was big money in those days.

I also had a job at the Northfield News on occasion doing job printing on the small press. The Linotype was a very difficult machine, but I had practice time every night. It was something new, and I was eager to learn. In the whole newspaper industry, you learned to read upside down and backwards.

During one summer, I worked at that National Music Camp at Interlachen. I had worked for the dietician at school, typing the menus every day. She later became the dietician for Interlachen.

I worked the storeroom at the camp. It was in the cellar, and I remember there were these eight bags of leaf of a certain spice. Whoever ordered eight bags, I don't know. It would take about one leaf for a meal and there were eight gunny sacks of the stuff.

One summer, I was employed at Mt. Pleasant, Michigan, at the Roosevelt Refinery Co. The president of that oil company had a daughter at Carleton who was very much enamored with a fellow. We approached the fellow and asked him if he could get a job for us for the summer, and he did.

We lived in town and hired a room. The three of us all shared the same bed. We covered the cracking tower for 24 hours, working different shifts. One of the fellows was sensitive to bed bugs, and he'd wake up in the middle of the night scratching like a mad dog. And another one of the guys was an oboist, and I got to play the oboe for the first time that summer.

On different levels on that tower, they would take off the resident from the crude. I suppose it would be diesel or kerosene and finally gasoline at the right time. The three of us managed a lab for eight hours each. We had to boil gasoline and measure the boiling points and take the results to the engineers on the cracking tower.

During the rest of the year, I lived at the college in the dormitory. I waited tables. In my senior year, they said I couldn't be head waiter or they'd start owing me money, and they don't like to do that. So I took a proctorship.

Sterrie was Conference champion in the 440 yard dash for Carleton during his senior year in 1938. He anchored Carleton's two-mile relay team that won the Chicago Relays that year.

My studies went well, and in 1939 I took honors in the field of Chemistry. I was president of the Senior Class and captain of the track team. I was a middle distance runner, and I only weighed about 135 lbs. in those days. Later, in the Navy, I got up to about 155 lbs.

I was conference champion in the 440-yard run during my senior year at Carleton. I even had my picture in the Chicago Tribune, winning the two-mile relay in the Chicago Relays in 1938. It was a great big picture of Norman. I ran the anchor leg, the last half mile. There were only four or five of us on the track team.

I came in second in the AAU meet in Minneapolis in 1938. I got knocked down on the take off, and I had to pick myself off the ground and then run like hell. Nobody was to blame, it was just the pack taking off. It's one of the hazards of track.

I was accepted into the fraternity at Carleton. At our first meeting we all voted to disband the organization. We saw no reason for that type of thing at Carleton.

When I graduated in 1939, I didn't have a job. Jobs were very difficult in those days. My major was chemistry. My closest friends in school all became doctors, so I must have been thinking about it. But there was no hope for going to medical school. My folks didn't have any money either, and they had three kids to educate yet.

At left, the St. James School. Sterrie was in the first class that went all the way through the school.

At right, the train station.

GROWING UP

BETSY BULLIS
Sociology   Minneapolis, Minn.

One of Minneapolis's nicest products, we proudly present Betsy — an all-round Carleton girl. She has played a part in most organizations and activities on campus—C.S.A. vice-president, freshman president of Gridley, Junior Head, C-in-C Board member, Phi Beta Kappa member, and Y.W.C.A. prexy are but a few examples. Next year she will do graduate work.

Sterrie met his future wife, Betsy Bullis, while at Carleton. She graduated Phi Beta Kappa, a fact that Sterrie said she often reminded him of in the years ahead.

NORMAN STERRIE
Chemistry   St. James, Minn.

"Norm" left his tracks in the symphony band, the dance band, and in the races. His last year, he acquired two letters, the honor of being track captain, a position as Proctor, senior class president, and the trials of taking honors in chemistry. His picture may be found in Evans A-31. Right, Betsy?

Sterrie, in addition to his other accomplishements at Carleton, was the senior class president.

The N2S trainer, designed by Stearman and built by Boeing, with Navy markings. It was painted a brilliant yellow and was known among the cadets as the "yellow peril."

Chapter Two
Training

Flight Training

When I graduated from Carleton, I didn't have in mind to be a doctor because I couldn't afford any more schooling. I thought I could become a chemist, but I quickly learned in my interviews with various company chemists that it would be very necessary to get a PhD in chemistry to get anyplace in that field.

At that time, it would have been an impossibility.

There were not a lot of jobs out there, and the Navy Flight Program looked very promising. I had a close college friend, who was also a chemist, and who had been in a Navy program for four years. He thought that was a great life for him. He had signed up for the Navy Reserve program, four years at ensign's pay. Plus, there was a bonus of $500 when you finished your four-year course as a naval aviator.

The war, of course, was impending. I had little question in my own mind that we would be in it. It was only a question of when.

I tried out for the Navy Aviation Cadet Program in July, 1939. There was an elimination process out at Wold-Chamberlain Field in Minneapolis. They had similar processes going on across the country – Seattle, Atlanta, Chicago, Boston, New York. The goal was to turn out a hundred pilots a month combined.

They told me it would be desirable to have a technical degree, and I had that. But the first step was the eye exam, and if you can't pass that, you're out. I passed it and got into the program.

There were six of us at Wold-Chamberlain. I think that's the number they took in at every base. Three of us made it. The Navy made me a seaman second class. You were given up to 10 hours instruction time leading up to soloing. We got to take the plane out by ourselves in the hayfields south of the airfield. I remember those high line wires going across town just south of the airport.

We flew N2S trainers, built by the Navy in Philadelphia. Everybody called them "yellow perils" because of how they were painted. The planes were twin-winged and canvas covered.

The next stop was Pensacola where the training was broken down into five phases, or "squadrons." Before you got into that, the first month was ground school. We learned about the engines and so on. It was October of 1939, and I was in Class 131C.

It was about that time that President Roosevelt came out with his "50,000 pilots a year" to be trained, and the construction of an equivalent number of planes. In the middle of that business, if you had it down, you were given another 10 hours of experience with a co-pilot trainer. The trouble was, you had a heck of a time finding an instructor because they were all soaked up in the 50,000-a-year bit. So students were stacked up, waiting to go on with their training.

There were so many Yellow Perils down at Pensacola, all coming and going at the same time. It was a cold winter down there, and we flew in very heavy flight suits. They were made of leather and sheepskin. And you were still cold.

The food was satisfactory. There was a lot of stuff I hadn't eaten before – southern cooking.
I began smoking at Pensacola. It was the only time in my life that I did. I quit after I got out of the Navy. I never smoked in college.

Squadron 1 was training in flying boats, but there weren't many planes available. The Navy had all of those planes down on the beach. I think they were in miserable condition anyway, the whole bay was littered with those flying boats. They needed mechanical help.

Squadron 2 was the beginning squadron at Corey Field. Half our time was spent in the plane, and the other half was spent on the ground, learning Morse code. When you finished a certain level with Morse code then you were allowed to use the full hour in the air. It took me three months or so to learn the code well, and I still know it. Some things never leave you. It came in handy later when I got my amateur radio license. I did it for a few years after the war.

I didn't have any threats to life while I was training. In Squadron 2, you had to land the plane in a 50-foot diameter circle, repeatedly, from about 3,000 feet. That was a technique that had to be learned. It was an exercise in precision flying.

Training

Norm took his flight training at NAS Pensacola, known as the "Cradle of Naval Aviation."

And then there was small field work, in a very small pasture. We had to fly these cumbersome, old, dilapidated airplanes. The field was surrounded with junk, people unable to get out. It was such foolishness, but we had to do it. That field was at Milton.

If you got to squadron 3, you figured you had made it. We had service-type planes. We had the twin-winged Vought for cross-country training, and they all had radial engines.

I once took a long-distance flight down to New Orleans from Pensacola. That was a big deal, following the coast all the way to New Orleans and following the coast all the way back. You made sure there were no clouds.

There were hurricane warnings once, and the Navy took all the planes out of Pensacola. The instructors would take them up north a couple of hundred miles.

Squadron 4 was acrobatics. For stunts and dog fighting, we had little ships, little bi-planes. All you had to do was hop in, and the tail wheel was set. You punched the throttle and off you went. They were fast little planes for their time. These were the types of planes they used to hook under dirigi-

Norm with his parents, Ella and Ole, in July 1940 while he was home on leave after getting his wings.

bles and release at altitude. There's one in the Smithsonian museum in Washington.

In Squadron 5, instrument training, the planes were single-wing, early ones with an elliptical end that were considered too dangerous. They had a low stalling speed. They were replaced by the perpendicular wing, but I can't think of the name of them.

I finished the course in June of 1940 in Pensacola, and I got my wings. A group of us were called into the commandant's office. I pinned my wings on myself.

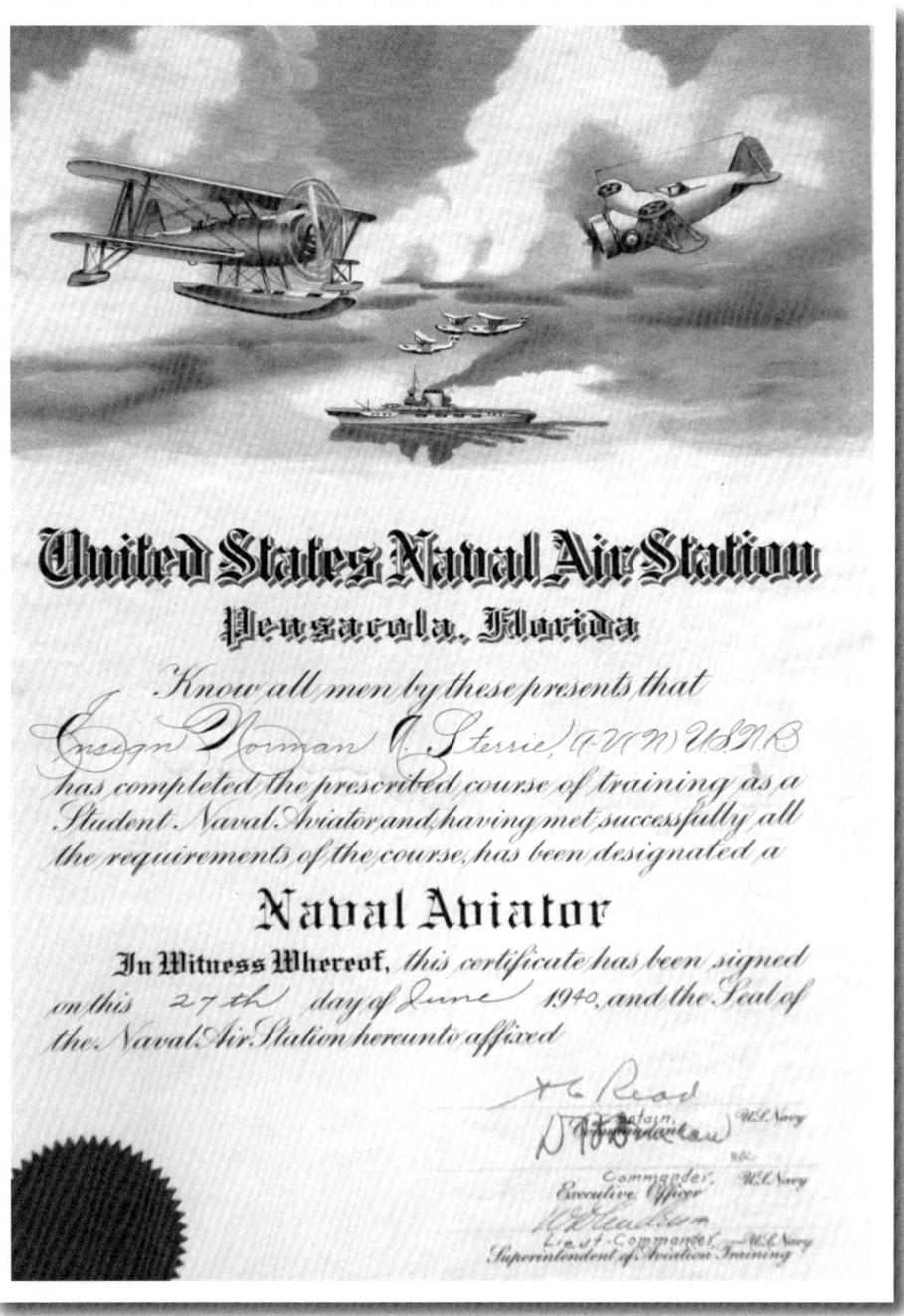

Norm earned his wings on June 27, 1940.

There were from 50 to 100 in our class to start, and most of them graduated. You had to buy a carton of cigarettes to give to the man who assigned you to the check pilots. If you wanted an easy check pilot, you forked over a carton of cigarettes to this man in the tower, and that's how that worked. Did I do it? Oh, yes. Everybody did that. Of course, if everybody did, I don't know what good it did except to give that guy a lot of cigarettes.

I was pretty nervous at first on that flight, but then I felt more at ease in the plane, and not so worried about the check.

You never knew what kind of plane you were going into until the week you graduated. It was a random assignment as far as I could tell. Very few people chose torpedo bombers, if any. Not the TBD Devastator anyway.

My orders when I graduated were to Torpedo Squadron 2 based on the USS Lexington, home-ported in California. Pilots didn't train on the planes they were flying until they went to the fleet. There weren't enough TBDs made to sacrifice in training programs.

The orignal USS Lexington, CV-2, just before the start of World War II.

Chapter Three
Going to War

Training with the Devastator

Sterrie reported to the USS Lexington in July of 1940 and started training on the Douglas TBD Devastator. The torpedo bomber had entered the service in 1937 as one of the most advanced planes in the world, but by the time the U.S. entered the war it was severely outdated.

In all, 130 Devastators were built. It had a maximum speed of 206 miles an hour, but usually flew at just over 100 miles an hour while carrying a torpedo. It had a crew of three: the pilot, the torpedo officer/navigator and a gunner/radioman.

The USS Lexington was home-ported in Long Beach, California, and I arrived in the summer of 1940. I had taken a train to Kansas City and then hitched a ride with a dive-bomber pilot the rest of the way. I reported to Naval Air Station, Coronado.

I was assigned to VT-2, the torpedo squadron aboard the Lex. The insignia for VT-2 was a dummy riding a torpedo. The tail on our TBDs was painted with stripes.

I believe I'm the last person alive to have ever flown the TBD Devastator in combat, and I've been asked many times what my impression of the Devastator was. It was a nice plane to fly. You could land either transport style or three-point style. It's a beautiful, Douglas-made, very wide-winged, radial-engined plane. I have copies of the brochure.

The problem was that it was a 100-mile-an-hour airplane in a 300-mile-an-hour war.

Sterrie referred to the patch for VT-2 as a "dummy riding a torpedo." Actually it was a bomb riding a torpedo.

Before I got to San Diego, I had never flown a Devastator. I read the book first, so I could find out where everything was.

They said in the book that the Devastator could reach a top speed of 206 miles per hour. Don't they wish. I did a speed run from Oceanside down to San Diego, plane empty, full throttle, and averaged 115 knots, or about 125 miles an hour. The only way the Devastator could reach 206 miles an hour was straight down.

Plus, it had a trick about it. The wings, which folded up for storage, had to be lowered and locked before takeoff. I never could understand why they lost so many planes because the pilots forgot to lock the wings before they took off. We had to go through our check-off list before every flight, but sometimes we were very sketchy about that. There was no indicator light that the wings weren't locked. Nothing. If you got in too much of a hurry, you would get killed when you tried to take off. A high school student could have designed something that would have told you whether they were locked.

I think the original contract was for 100 of the TBDs. It was designed for a pilot and gunner, far back. We had a 30-caliber machine gun, and the center seat was equipped with a pilot stick, so there could be a second pilot. We took that out, and gave the middle man a rifle. We always tried to have three in the plane, but some squadrons only had the pilot and the gunner. The guy with the rifle could keep busy – aiming. What else could you give him? There's nothing back there.

We learned carrier landings in the fleet. We practiced on the Lexington or on the Sara (USS Saratoga) which was the sister ship of the Lex, also based either in Long Beach or San Diego.

I don't remember my first carrier landing. There have been so many since. It was up in the hundreds. I do remember the last one, which was in the Philippine Sea at night. Couldn't see a damn thing except the flags and lining up the ship. What a relief when I cut the gun and when the tail hook grabbed. I was safely

The Douglas TBD Devastator was "a 100-mile-an-hour airplane in a 300-mile-an-hour war."

aboard. Actually that wasn't my last landing, it was the last one I remember.

In the late fall of 1940, we went out to Honolulu, to Hawaii. We were there for several months before returning to San Diego. For the next year, we were always practicing, group practice, squadron practice, individual practice. We had the dive bombers, the torpedo planes and the fighters aboard. I remember the little fighters. The pilot had to crank up the wheels after takeoff.

I wasn't surprised at how slow the Devastator was. You had what you had. The attention of the whole world was on the war in Europe, and so if we needed an extra screw or nail or anything, it could be a problem. We did have the top secret Norden bombsight installed in the TBD, and we had to strictly account for it at the end of each flight. We had to turn it back in for safety.

The pilot generally does the navigating in the Devastator, but if you're on a mission and doing high-level bombing, like from 10 or 12-thousand feet, the second-seat man can go down into a little place where he could look through a little hole and set the Norden bombsight. With that, he could focus on the target. He had control of the airplane – lateral control at least.

On the ship, we had our own cabin. Junior officers had their own dining room – that is, ensigns like me. Lieutenant junior grade went to the big dining room. We weren't allowed up there. We were okay with that. The nation was counting on us to win the war, not those old geezers upstairs.

Our dining room was our ready room too. There were four squadrons all trying to learn and do the same thing. It was ridiculous. We'd sit at different tables and try to concentrate.

GETTING MARRIED

Betsy, my future wife, was a fellow student at Carlton, and she was a college sweetheart. We met in the early stages of our education, and it never went away. She went on to become a Phi Beta Kappa, which I had to live with throughout our married life.

She was very bright, of course – a Minneapolis girl, Central High School. I never met her father, who was killed in an accident when he was walking across the street and got hit by some college kids going home for Thanksgiving – they were not at fault.

I learned to like and to be very appreciative of her mother and her mother's family. They were a Long Lake inheritance. Betsy was a very good student and had a major in social work. She, like I, worked her way through school.

After graduation, she became a social worker for Hennepin County. This put certain demands on her. I remember coming home from the Navy at one time, and they had a big parade in St. James. I was the centerpiece of that parade, and Bets could not attend because of her social work needs in the county.

That all ended after the war when we bought our house and I was in medical school. We had the youngster at our home out by the Vets Hospital.

We got married just before the war in September of 1941. I was home-based in San Diego, and the ship came into port. We were going to have leave, probably a fairly long leave that I could predict. I urged her to come out.

We took a two-week trip up to San Francisco and saw the big national park up that way. We returned to Coronado where I had rented a very small house that later became the office of the chamber of commerce of the city.

One thing led to another, and we decided to get married. We got married in Yuma, Arizona. California had a three-day waiting period of some kind, and you

Norm and Betsy in Coronado in September, 1941, at the time of their marriage.

Norm and Betsy on their trip to Yosemite, just prior to their marriage in 1941.

had to have blood tests and that sort of thing. So we went to Yuma and looked up a preacher, knocked on his door, and asked if he would marry us. He rounded up a couple of neighbors to witness the ceremony. That was our marriage. Yuma was one of the marriage capitals, along with Reno.

The wives of the squadron all had reservations on a liner to Hawaii so they could join us when the Lexington pulled in there. The Lex would be based out of Honolulu and would be in and out of the islands. But the reservations all kept canceling as the war effort became apparent. One after another, the cancellations came through. She never made it to Hawaii and went back home to Minnesota.

Our daughter was born in January of 1944. Her name is Margaret. During the war, the family lived in Minneapolis at 3812 Park Avenue.

PEARL HARBOR

We rotated with the USS Enterprise before the attack on Pearl Harbor in late 1941 – ten days each, ten in and ten out from Hawaii. They were coming in, and we were heading out when Pearl Harbor was hit.

They were due in just as the Japanese attacked. In fact one of their planes – flown by a St. Paul boy, Mac something – was shot down during the attack by our ground forces.

The Japanese did us a favor by taking out those battleships. I don't know why they were all in a line there, but they were targeted for destruction that's for sure.

When we found out the Japanese had hit Pearl Harbor, there was supposed to be a group practice that day. We were all standing around and nothing seemed to be happening. We all wondered, what the hell was happening? When do we go? All of a sudden, the door opened, and the Squadron 2 skipper appeared at the door. He said, "The exercise has been called off. The Japanese have just hit Pearl Harbor, and we are changing to live ammunition." That meant bombs, guns, everything – live. That was our introduction to war. We sat there, kind of stunned.

At the time we were about 400 miles off Midway. We were taking a Marine group out to the island. There was some thought of going after the Japanese fleet. We waited for information. Where could they be? But there was no information from any scouting planes. Finally, a B-17 on the way to Johnston Island reported a carrier on that route. So we turned to the south to intercept, but we later got the news it was a garbage scow or something.

We were sent out looking for submarines in our Avengers. We divided the search into sectors. We went out 200 miles and returned. We did that ahead of the carrier when it was at sea. The idea was to sweep the area clean. Every day we had a search sector.

Six Japanese carriers and their squadrons of war planes attacked Pearl Harbor on the morning of Dec. 7, 1941. The attack sank four major U.S. battleships and damaged four more. Over 2,400 American servicemen were killed.

The United States had three carriers in the Pacific at that time: USS Enterprise, USS Lexington and USS Saratoga.

The Enterprise was just returning from bringing a Marine squadron to Wake Island, and was 215 miles from Oahu when the attack began. The Lexington was bringing a Marine squadron to Midway and was 500 miles south of that island on December 7. Saratoga had recently been overhauled at the shipyard in Bremerton, Washington, and had returned to San Diego.

The other carriers, USS Yorktown, USS Wasp, USS Ranger and USS Hornet were all in the Atlantic.

GOING TO WAR

The USS Arizona burns and sinks after the attack on Pearl Harbor, Dec. 7, 1941.

One day I encountered a submarine on my search leg. As soon as I spotted it, I went to full throttle – now the question was: ours or theirs? We had a signal, making a left circle, to indicate we were a friendly. I started that circle, and, lo and behold, he took a shot at me from his front cannon. That decided that question. I was full throttle to him, and I saw a Japanese sailor scurry to the conning tower and quickly dive in. I proceeded on course, but the plane was just too slow. The sub had submerged by the time we got to it. We dropped our depth charges where he might have been. The second plane in my formation also made a dive on him, but to no avail. We could have been war heroes right from the start.

When we finally got back to Pearl Harbor, we were shocked. It was just sheer devastation. We were only going to be in port for a few days, but they were going to give the pilots a night at the Royal Hawaiian. The Navy had taken over the hotel. I remember getting a room and looking at the little card that said how much it cost. It was $50 a night. Can you imagine staying at a place that cost $50 a night? I was making about $75 a month, plus flight pay.

In the middle of the night, there was a knock at the door and a military policeman told me to get

Butch O'Hare and Sterrie both served aboard the Lex in early 1942. O'Hare earned his Medal of Honor while flying off the carrier.

Edward "Butch" O'Hare transferred aboard the USS Lexington on Jan. 31, 1942, just a few weeks after the attack at Pearl Harbor. Three weeks later, he became one of the most famous airmen of World War II.

On Feb. 20, a group of nine Japanese bombers was approaching the Lexington, and only O'Hare and his wingman were available for protection. O'Hare's wingman had to drop out of the attack because his guns were jammed, and so the Chicago-born pilot took on the nine "Bettys," twin-engined bombers, himself. At close range, again and again, O'Hare charged at the bombers, his machine guns blazing. In his official citation, O'Hare was given credit for shooting down five of the bombers and damaging another. In one day, he became America's first ace in the Pacific.

A hero, he left the ship in March and spent time doing war-bond tours and receiving his Medal of Honor from President Roosevelt. He returned to combat in late 1943 and distinguished himself again as an aggressive and tactically superior fighter pilot. O'Hare became commander of an entire air group, and led the first American night fighter mission of the war on Nov. 26, 1943. He was shot down and killed while attacking a group of enemy bombers. O'Hare International Airport in Chicago is named after him.

up and get out. He said, "We're taking you back to Pearl Harbor." Someone had reported a submarine in the harbor, and the Lexington was getting underway. So we sped out to Pearl, going 50 miles an hour with no lights. Then the Navy canceled getting underway. But there went my night at the Royal Hawaiian.

Not long after Pearl Harbor, Butch O'Hare came aboard. He was in the fighter squadron on the Lexington. He was a very nice guy and a hero. They took him on a war bond tour of the United States. Later, he developed a carrier night-fighter squadron, but on one of his attacks, as he was approaching a Japanese bomber they got to him first. I don't know how it happened, but we heard about it right away. It was a sad loss. His father was an attorney for Al Capone, but we never talked about that.

Salamaua and Lae

The Lexington was covering the approaches to Australia in early March, 1942. Word came that there was an assembly of Japanese ships up at Salamaua and Lae on the north coast of New Guinea. Orders came through that we were to attack that group and break up any landings the Japanese had in mind.

It seems to me that there was not much going on in the war at that time, as far as the Navy was concerned. The word came down that America needs heroes. It was decided that our formation would attack the Japanese assembling in the harbor at Salamaua-Lae.

We were in the seas east of Australia. The plan was to attack that bunch, but we had to go over the Owen Stanley Mountains to get there. We asked everybody, has anybody ever gone up to 12,000 feet with a torpedo on this plane? Nobody knew. We decided to try it anyway. This was our first mission.

The group commander, William B. Ault, was sent into Port Moresby to get details of the terrain and its surroundings. The information he brought back was delivered from stencils, probably using old National Geographic maps. It was very crude anyway. It was apparent that we were going to have to go over the mountains through a narrow pass. The pass closed over about noon every day with clouds.

In preparation, the group commander was going to be stationed up over the pass, and while we were going up and down the other side, he would keep track as to whether the pass was open or if it closed.

It came time for the attack on March 10, and there would be no problems for the fighters and dive bombers to go up to that altitude, but the question was whether the torpedo planes with their 2,000 lb. torpedo could go that high and over the pass. Nobody had ever done it before.

The only thing to do was try it. We had oxygen for altitude flying, but that was it.

The Japanese occupied Salamaua and Lae in Papua, New Guinea, in March 1942.

In an effort to stop the occupation, U.S. Naval forces, including the carriers Yorktown and Lexington, gathered on the south side of Papua. With help from 16 land based bombers, the aircraft from the carriers attacked the Japanese position at Salamaua and Lae on March 10.

The Lexington launched its planes, including VT-2, the torpedo squadron, at 7:49 a.m. that morning, and the Yorktown launched 11 minutes later.

Planes had to travel 201 kilometers over the Owen Stanley Range in order to get to the north side of the Papua penninsula and the targets.

The Lexington's bombers and torpedo planes attacked at 9:38 a.m. and the Yorktown's contingent followed shortly thereafter. There were 104 planes in the attack, and 103 of them made it back to the carriers safely by noon.

The attack did not stop the occupation, but it did sink three transport ships and damaged a host of others.

Salamaua and Lae were eventually recaptured by MacArthur and the Allied forces in the summer of 1943.

The group took off, and as we approached the pass, from my view at the tail end of the formation at least, they flew up to the pass and kept going and going, and I thought, "When are we going to turn around?" It was very apparent they weren't going to make it.

At the last moment, the torpedo skipper, Jimmy Brett, made a very sharp turn and reversed his course. We proceeded about five to ten miles back from where we started in order to renew the climb. As we approached this time, it was apparent it was going to be very close. We did proceed over the pass, clearing the terrain by 50 to 100 feet at the most. I saw details of rudimentary shacks underneath as we went over. We were much too close to the ground as far as I was concerned.

Once reaching the other side, it was a descent for the next five or ten miles to sea level. As we approached the enemy in the harbor, I was very close to the shoreline. This was our very first mission, and I had a certain amount of fear. Behind every tree lurked a potential Japanese with a machine gun surely.

As we approached the harbor, the dive bombers went in and likewise the torpedo planes. We were right on their tail. We were probably at 50 to 100 feet. I noticed only two or three vessels as targets. They were destroyers. We expected more, but that was all there was.

We went in and made our drops at probably 50 feet and quickly got out of there without knowing

The Owen Stanley Range on the way to Salamaua-Lae.

Devastators from the Yorktown cleared the pass and prepared for an attack in Huon Gulf near Salamaua and Lae. Japanese ships in the bay are making smoke to hide themselves from the aircraft. U.S. Navy photo.

whether the torpedoes were in the mud below us or were on their way. I saw no evidence of anything hitting at any rate.

I found myself rather alone at the tail end of this formation. It was not a comfortable feeling with everyone else turning around before I could even begin. I made my drop pursuing this one vessel that had made for the outlet to the harbor. I was under fire all the way in, of course. I made my drop, turned around and headed back for the pass. The way to avoid the anti-aircraft fire was to use a technique called jinking. You'd go up a few feet, maybe 50 feet, and then down again. Then you'd go side to side, never being a target for more than two or three seconds at a time. On the turn to get out, you bared your whole silhouette, and that was perhaps a touchy moment for you.

The pass had not closed, and the group, minus one dive bomber, which had been shot down, arrived at the pass, made it over, and headed back to the other side and safely landed shortly thereafter. Such was the battle for Salamaua-Lae.

I got the Navy Cross on the recommendation of the squadron commander. At that point of the war, the Japanese were up and down the coast of India and raising all kinds of trouble in the Indian Ocean with merchant ships. There had been no action on the part of the U.S. And, as I said, the word came down: America needs heroes.

I'm not sure if all of us got a Navy Cross, and I don't know how you could judge any difference between us. From one report, there were 12 torpedoes dropped in the harbor. There may have been dive-bomber hits, but as for the torpedoes, we just don't know if they did any damage.

That was the first of 35 missions I flew. We had no previous combat experience. You don't know what you're up against. It was strange territory. Everybody was nervous about the whole business. Going out on a combat mission, you were nervous whether it was number one or number 35.

A Devastator comes in for a carrier landing in July 1942. U.S. Navy photograph.

You're so keyed up for the whole business, not knowing what's going to happen or whether you're going to make it or not.

It's like waiting for the gun to go off at a track meet. Bang goes the gun, and off you go. All nervousness is gone. As you're revving up to go down the deck, everything is now directed toward flying the airplane. No nervousness.

On getting back, when that hook grabs the wire, you kind of take a deep breath and say to yourself, "I made it again." You get out of the landing area so that the following plane, less than 50 or 60 seconds later, has a place to drop.

I can't speak for the other guys, but once the ship was in sight and you were in the landing circle, you had to be sharp for that landing. Once you are grabbed by the tail hook, it's a huge sense of relief and the shaking is over.

I don't remember that I ever missed a cable. You do remember the difficult ones, or those that became difficult.

The maneuverability of our little planes in comparison to the big ships today was extraordinary. There's just no comparison. We had a lot of control coming in. With the TBD, we came in about 50 knots or so, maybe 60. It was very slow.

They like to have the carrier going 20, maybe 25 knots over the bow. So you're landing at a difference of maybe 40 or 50 miles an hour. But you'd better be set up right at the last moment. I think there were five or six cables. The last one was a barrier. It was up in the air three or four feet. There was no touch and go. They were going to capture you no matter what, and the final "what" was the barrier. The Landing Signal Officer was there to try to prevent that sort of thing. You had no business being up in the air that high at that point anyway. In some of the crash landings you see, they're ramming into one of the gun turrets on the right side.

It was exciting to watch carrier landings. When you weren't flying yourself, generally you'd go up and watch them. One place we could watch them was right behind the Landing Signal Officer on the landing deck. You positioned yourself so you weren't in the way of anything falling or being propelled at you. Your eyeballs were at deck level, but the rest of you was below the landing deck. Sometimes we'd go up on the superstructure and watch them, but it wasn't as exciting as watching them on the deck level.

After a mission, we nearly always went up to the bridge first to see Task Force 58, Admiral Marc Mitscher. The pilots would talk to him before they ever talked to the intelligence people. It was just his way. He wanted to know first-hand before anybody else got to you what the story was. We'd go up as a group sometimes, and sometimes alone. We didn't talk to reporters after the mission. At one point we had Stanley Johnston, a famous war correspondent aboard. He was an Australian. He didn't talk to the pilots very much. I think he talked to the Admiral and all the big shots.

Grover's Work

As I said, as far as I know I'm the last TBD pilot left who flew in combat. There could be somebody from the old Yorktown, I don't know. Probably not. I was interviewed by a film production company in Portland, Oregon, a couple of years ago. They had found a crew that they said was the last crew of a TBD, but later on I got a call from one of crew that flew with me on the Lexington, so I know that's not true. The man who called was a fellow by the name of Cosgrove, E.D. Cosgrove. We called him Grover. One of the crewmen I met in Portland said he remembered that name. He also remembered the incident when Grover shot off my tail.

There was a fighter after me, and this machine gun cut right through the tail of my Devastator. It

THE SECRETARY OF THE NAVY

WASHINGTON

The President of the United States takes pleasure in presenting the NAVY CROSS to

LIEUTENANT NORMAN A. STERRIE
UNITED STATES NAVAL RESERVE

for service as set forth in the following

CITATION:

"For distinguished service in the line of his profession as a pilot of Torpedo Squadron TWO, when, on March 10, 1942, in enemy waters, Ensign Sterrie participated in a vigorous and determined dive bombing attack, in the face of heavy anti-aircraft fire, on enemy ships, and as a result of this attack at least one ship was sunk."

For the President,

Frank Knox
Secretary of the Navy.

Sterrie's first Navy Cross came for his work at Salamaua and Lae.

could have been dire circumstances, but I didn't realize it at the time. Grover didn't say anything. Later, after we landed, I saw the tail was pretty well shot up, but I thought it was from the Japanese flier attacking me. But it was Grover's work. A gun mounted on a turret would have an interrupter so you couldn't hit the tail, but he was using a free gun in back.

After I went to my cabin, that afternoon or night, the chief came up and said he wanted to put Grover on report for a captain's mast, a naval court. I said, "No way, he probably saved my life." Anybody who rides in my backseat, shooting at the enemy, is on my side.

A devastating explosion wracked the once-mighty Lexington in the Battle of the Coral Sea. She sank on May 8, 1942. U.S. Navy photo.

Chapter Four
Battle of the Coral Sea

The Japanese were into the Indian Ocean and along the coast of Burma. Leading up to the Battle of the Coral Sea, we were on station south of New Guinea, and we knew that the Japanese were aware of our presence there.

I guess they assumed we were a good target. The Battle of the Coral Sea took two days and involved the carriers Lexington and Yorktown. The Yorktown had been ordered to join the Lexington to protect the approaches to Australia.

Day one involved the Yorktown finding the enemy carrier and its support group near Tulagi. It was a Japanese support carrier of some kind, not a major ship. They reported to the fleet the presence of this carrier in the harbor around Tulagi.

Orders were given the following day to find and attack that carrier. I suppose a position report had been given. We launched our full complement. It was a bright, sunshiny day. We had about 60 planes: dive bombers, fighters, torpedo bombers. We had 12 planes in Torpedo 2.

As we neared the ship, there was dense smoke coming up. We observed that the ship obviously had been a target of something. As we approached, we lined up. We were strung out in preparation for an attack. I was tail-end Charlie. I was apparently the junior guy.
As we neared the Japanese carrier, I noticed a solitary seaplane fighter, and he was making an attack on me. My gunner fired at him as he was diving down. Our squadron was headed in the same

Death of a Carrier

The Lexington, a 43,000-ton aircraft carrier, was the fourth ship of its name, dating to the American Revolution. Its identifier was CV-2, the second modern aircraft carrier, although it was actually built on the hull of a cruiser. It was commissioned in 1927 as a sister ship of the USS Saratoga.

Lexington was a huge ship, 888 feet long by 106 feet wide. The flight deck was made of splinter-resistant teak wood. The island on the starboard side was built fore and aft of a massive stack and was counter-weighted by fuel tanks on the port side of the ship. Lexington was driven by four huge engines that could create 180,000 horsepower through four gigantic screws. The ship, big as it was, could race through the water at 35 knots or about 40 miles per hour. It could even go 25 knots in reverse.

In contrast to later carriers that relied on their destroyer screen and their air wing for protection, CV-2 was heavily armed with 8-inch and 5-inch guns.

The USS Lexington was built in Massachussets and was sometimes called the Gray Lady or the Lady Lex. It could travel 2,200 miles in 72 hours. In 1929, during an emergency, it supplied electricity to the city of Tacoma, Wash., for three weeks.

direction as the opposing fleet. Later, that seaplane was shot down by our fighters.

When you went in, you had your speed and, of course, you had to have the ship's direction and speed to understand where you wanted to drop. But we had kind of a hay rake thing on top of the instrument panel. Can you imagine screwing around with that? This damn hay rake, you'd jiggle it around, what direction is the boat going, and how fast am I going? Imagine putting up with that when shells are bursting all over you.

So mostly we just eyeballed it. We tried to figure out how much to lead it with our torpedoes just by looking. At the Coral Sea, it was easy the first day because the ship was almost standing still.

I had a broadside attack on the ship. I later learned that the ship was sunk and at least five torpedoes went into her. The carrier was obviously impaired as I was heading in. I did not see any opposing fire, although I suspect there was some.

Our altitude was about 100 feet, and we were going full bore. In those planes, that was 100 knots. We were all lined up against him. It was during that attack and later that Lt. Commander Robert Dixon of Bombing 2 reported that the carrier was sinking: "Scratch one flattop."

After you let go of your torpedo, you get the hell out of there. You have your escape plan before you head in. This doesn't sound very exciting, but the 12 of us got back to the ship, and I don't think there was any further incident that day. But there were huge mistakes made on the part of both opponents. We later learned that the Japanese had sunk our oiler and its supporting destroyer. Their mistake came at night when they made an attempt to land on our carriers.

The opponents were very close to each other that night. We knew we were in for trouble the next day because the opposing ships could not have been more than 70 miles apart. Even though we knew what was coming, we were still rejoicing over the kill we had done on that day.

The Lexington's planes hit the stranded Shoho with several torpedoes and may have dealt the carrier the final blow. She sank a half-hour after the attack. U.S. Navy photo.

Morning came. We were waiting for the scouts, and they had been sent out very early. The first side to locate the enemy would be in a very advantageous position. Our call came late that morning. I think Joe Smith of Scouting 2 made the sighting report.

We all took off. Bombing 2 took off without us and never looked back. Normally they would have waited so we could have made a combined attack, but those suckers just took off and left us.

We went to where the report said they were, and no ships were found. We wondered what was wrong. It was a bad position report. Our skipper decided to do an expanding box to locate them. We were at about two thousand or three thousand feet, and you could see 20 miles or so. We should have been able to at least pick up the wakes of the enemy ships from that distance.

After we had started doing the box, using up our precious fuel, our group commander said the fleet was approximately 40 miles from where they had said they were. That was Group Commander William Ault, a fine gentleman who was having his own battle

In 1937, the ship was involved in the search for Amelia Earhart.

Designed for a crew of 2,200, the ship had nearly 3,000 on board as it went to war. It carried 18 fighters, 36 dive bombers and 12 torpedo planes. Its skipper was Capt. Carl "Ted" Sherman, known both for his tough discipline and for his dog and constant companion, "Admiral Wags."

On May 1, 1942, the Lexington moved into the Coral Sea and joined the USS Yorktown as part of Task Force 17. They were hunting Japanese carriers, and the Japanese carriers were hunting them. In fact, there were three enemy carriers in the neighborhood: the Shokaku, Zuikako and the light carrier Shoho.

On May 7, the air group attacked and sank Shoho, and Lt. Commander Bob Dixon uttered the famous words, "Scratch one flattop." Meanwhile the Japanese sank the oiler Neosho and the destroyer Sims. The Coral Sea is remembered as the first naval battle in history where the ships never actually saw each other.

Also on that day, eight Japanese planes tried to land on the Lexington, and had received the signal to land, when they were driven off by fire from the cruisers and destroyers nearby. From the air, all carriers tend to look alike.

Sterrie earned his second Navy Cross by attacking the Japanese carrier Shokaku in the Battle of the Coral Sea. Norm had already dropped his torpedo, but went in again with his skipper in order to draw off some of the anti-aircraft fire.

May 8th dawned hot and humid, about 97 degrees. Planes waited patiently on the deck until finally at 8:20 a report came in that the Japanese fleet was 120 miles north, later revised to 175 miles north. Both the Lex and the Yorktown launched, and both ships went to general quarters.

Yorktown's bombers and torpedo planes were able to find the target and bombed an enemy carrier. Lexington's planes couldn't find the enemy ships and started flying a search pattern, called a box, and soon found a damaged enemy carrier, smoking away.

Meanwhile, back at the mother ship, the first Japanese planes were spotted at 10:48 a.m. The Lexington launched the fighters it had remaining and sped up to 25 knots. At 11:18, the first torpedo hit the Lexington at about frame 50 on the port side. Two

with Zeroes — Japanese fighters. His supporting fighters, I think there were two or three with him, were shot down.

We stopped expanding the box and found the fleet where he said they were. The weather, fortunately for us, was rain with scattered clouds. We had no trouble finding them, and, in making our descent through holes in the clouds, we again strung out our formation to drop our torpedoes. I found myself now as the wing on the Torpedo 2 skipper, Jimmy Brett.

This time we were heading in the opposite direction that the ships were going. The skipper made a very sharp turn. I anticipated that he was making his drop, and I followed him on the tail end of the Japanese formation and dropped my torpedo. The ship I was attacking was turning one way, and I was coming in the other way.

It turned out the skipper never dropped his torpedo. We had attacked from a poor position and he decided he wanted a better shot at the opposing fleet. We went around the tail end of their fleet, and he decided to go in alone.

I was about two hundred or three hundred yards on his left. The two of us went in against the carrier and minutes later a second torpedo hit nearby.

In all, there were 100 Japanese planes in on the attack, and the Lex was also hit by five bombs, the most destructive of which exploded just ahead of the island. The whole attack lasted less than nine minutes.

Fires were burning throughout the ship, and below decks three of the 16 boilers had been knocked out by flooding. A seven-degree list was soon corrected by shifting ballast in the hull. Within a short time, the flight deck had been cleared, full speed was available, and the ship was ready to recover aircraft. The only major problem was that both elevators were stuck in the up position and could not be budged. Planes could not be brought below to the hangar deck.

The carrier managed to land some of its planes, refuel a few of them, and launch them again, waiting for the Japanese to attack once more. For a while, it seemed like the ship was going to make it.

At 12:47 p.m., however, there was a tremendous explosion below decks, and at 1:19 p.m. another blast ripped through the ship. The future of the carrier now looked grim, but Captain Sherman turned the carrier toward Australia, hoping to cover the 700 miles or so with a day's hard steaming.

numerous other ships. Their formation had turned around, too. We went in against a withering fire. We were jinking to avoid the fire.

As our dive brought us toward the water, I started noticing rough air. These were slip streams from the five-inch guns. I remember thinking, "When is he going to drop his torpedo? Drop it for gosh sakes." This went on for a few seconds, and I figured we'd better get out of there, which I did. I had nothing to drop anyway. The skipper was waiting to drop his, which he finally did. He got out, too.

I went in that second time to give the Japanese two targets to shoot at rather than one. I'd never do that again. That was a damn fool stunt. The two of us were taking on the whole damn fleet, and we both escaped.

After that last attack, we managed to corral the others in the group. There were 11 of us headed back. One of the pilots had mechanical trouble on the mission and elected to go back to the carrier earlier.

The aircraft were all neatly parked at the stern of the flight deck after the attack on the Lexington. The smoke was swirling around them. U.S. Navy photo.

At 2 p.m., the remaining planes returned and were recovered. They had inflicted further damage on the carrier Shokaku.

The crew fought bravely to keep the ship moving and to quell the fires, but at 2:43 p.m. there was another catastrophic explosion, this time just under the forward elevator. The blast dropped the elevator down a foot, and then it surged upward.

On the bridge, the officers lost control of steering the ship, while in the engineering compartments, temperatures were over 150 degrees. Lexington was still able to maintain 17 knots, and her destroyer escorts gathered close around her. At 4 p.m., the ship came to a dead halt, and the list on the deck increased. All squadron personnel were ordered aft, where they huddled in the rancid smoke beside their planes.

It was now clear to everyone on board that the next order would be to abandon ship, and at 5:07 p.m. Fleet Admiral Aubrey Fitch turned to Captain Sherman and said, "Well, Ted, it's time to get the boys off the ship."

The men began to climb ropes down the sides or to simply dive into the warm water. The seas were moderate. There was little panic, but the officers did try to slow the men down by barking through their bullhorns that the ship was not sinking.

The Japanese later reported there were no underwater explosions, which made us wonderful torpedo managers. Our skipper reported, I don't know on what grounds, that we had five hits. There were none that I saw. But you really can't see after you release your torpedo. You're just getting out of there.

We had a long ways to go to get back to the Lex. We had expended a lot of fuel in that expanding box, and now we were on a direct course home. About half way back, to our port side, perhaps a mile or two away, were the Japanese headed back to their ships after having hit ours. I noticed a couple of them breaking off from the main group as if they were headed our way. Others in our group saw the same thing.

You have never seen a tighter formation flying anywhere. We were flying at 50 to 100 feet altitude so they couldn't approach us from below. The planes that had been approaching us got called back – apparently they just wanted to leave well enough alone.

As we neared our own fleet, maybe a mile or two out, there was a heavy bombardment from our own ships. The sky was just black with anti-aircraft fire. What a reception. But we were long overdue and presumed lost. In any case, we were in the middle of their barrage. Somebody finally called that off.

As we approached the Lexington we noticed she was underway and making good speed, but trailing very dense black smoke. Obviously she had been damaged by something. We made our approaches and landed. All 11 of us returned. As I landed, I was directed to the forward elevator. We did a dipstick check at that point on our gas tank, and it didn't register anything.

I was about to get away from my plane, and BOOM. A terrific explosion sent me, and the elevator, and my plane – I was just about to hop off the thing – at least four feet up in the air. The whole elevator went up. That explosion led to the doom of the Lexington.
I made an attempt to get to my cabin, and I had to go down a couple of decks. It was tough going. On the way down, I had to pass a gun emplacement where someone had stacked at least a dozen bodies, all

The Lexington's captain called "abandon ship" at 5:07 p.m. on May 8. The men descended by ropes into the water where lifeboats and rafts waited. U.S. Navy photo.

killed by bomb or torpedo below decks. I never made it to my stateroom. The crew members were down there trying to wall off the exploding gasoline fumes. They certainly were brave men who had to know the inner parts of that ship.

I made my way back to the stern where others were gathered. I stayed on deck for the rest of the afternoon. It was a long wait. We wondered why on earth they didn't call for "abandon ship." The ship wasn't listing appreciably, but we sat on the back of the ship inhaling that dense smoke for several hours. At first they had to take the wounded off to a destroyer on one side.

Finally the order came to abandon ship, and there was a real scurry. But this time there was a list toward the port side. I ran for my plane and got a three-man life raft out. I lowered it down, but before I could even jump in the water, the raft was full of desperate people trying to get aboard. There was no room as I

With most of the men in the water or in lifeboats or life rafts, another huge explosion wracked the Lexington at 5:30 p.m. and then another at 5:37. The 50 planes on the stern began to catch fire and then explode, one by one, until the entire rear of the flight deck was red and yellow with flames.

At 6:30 p.m., Sherman took one last look around and felt sure that he was the last man alive aboard the carrier. He also took his leave of the stricken ship.

There were more than 500 of the Lexington's crew on the cruiser USS Minneapolis, 478 on the USS Hammann, and hundreds more on the USS New Orleans.

In her death throes, the Lexington lists severely to port. The crew, those who lived, were safely off the carrier. U.S. Navy photo.

Other escort ships picked up their share.

The ships cleared the area, nervous that the burning Lex would attract another Japanese attack. Only the USS Phelps was left behind – with orders to put the coup de grace to the carrier. The Phelps pumped three torpedoes into the Lexington. When the big ship continued to drift in the water, The Phelps put two more torpedoes into the other side.

Serenely, the Lexington slipped under the waves at 7:56 p.m., but she wasn't quite ready to go quietly into that good night. She had just disappeared below the waves when her torpedo warheads blew up. It was the biggest explosion of all, lifting the Phelps nearly out of the

saw.

So I went to another plane and got another life raft, and this time got one of my friends to go down with it and to hold it until I got there. As I made my descent down the rope about 50 feet, and got to the water, there was no room in that life raft for me either. It was full of people. I managed to get hold of one of the lines and hung on to the raft. We were surrounded by lifeboats from the surrounding ships. They were milling in and out, picking up anybody they could find. There was no oil on the water, just people.

Finally I got lifted aboard a lifeboat from the USS New Orleans. I was taken to that ship, climbed up the ladder and was safely aboard. All I had with me was a revolver. I don't know what I was going to do with that. I had my shoes tied to my vest, and the clothes on my back. I guess that's all everybody had.

On the deck, I encountered all kinds of wounded people from the Lexington. They were all wrapped up. I knew they wouldn't be around long – burned people. I left my clarinet, which I could not get to, and all my personal belongings, including a bottle of Scotch. Betsy and I had been married just before the ship took off from Hawaii, and all of the wedding gifts and kitchenware and so forth were in my stateroom. I had no need for all of that, but I really missed my clarinet. I had bought it before my last year in college. It was a very good instrument. It got replaced after the war through a gift – another fine clarinet – from my mother-in-law.

One of the ship's officers on the New Orleans gave me his stateroom for the night. There were two of us sharing that stateroom.

There were more than 2,000 survivors. The whole fleet was ordered to go to Tonga to reassemble. We went there, and on the way we were transferred to a destroyer. All of us who were transferred, of course, were land lubbers, not used to rolling around all of the time, and we were half-sick all the way there. We got to British Tonga and it seems to me the battleship South Dakota had gone aground there.

And that was the Battle of the Coral Sea.

When the battle was over, two Japanese carriers were made unusable for the upcoming Battle of Midway. The absence of those ships helped shape the Battle of Midway. I suppose the Naval Academy boys are still refighting that war today.

A Stop at New Caledonia

The torpedo pilots on the Lexington had left their planes on the sinking ship, and we were ordered back to San Diego to reassemble. I remember that on Tonga, our first stop, they took all of the young women away to the hills.

Torpedo Squadron 2 got orders to return to Fiji and New Caledonia. We took several days. The squadron was split up, and half went to Fiji and half to New Caledonia. We were five days on a munitions ship, traveling alone without any escort. It was a little different to be the target, but we made it back. I and three others, including the exec of the squadron,

water. USS New Orleans, 14 miles away, was shaken by the final death throes of the carrier.

Lexington went down 200 miles south of Rossel Island in 2,000 fathoms, more than two miles deep. Of her crew of nearly 3,000, 216 were lost.

Most of the above information came from:
The Lexington Goes Down: The Last Seven Hours of a Fighting Lady
A.A. Hoehling
Prentice-Hall, New Jersey, 1971

From the deck of a nearby cruiser, sailors could see the burning Lexington as it was wracked by another explosion. U.S. Navy photo.

made it to New Caledonia, which was a French protectorate. The reason we were sent back to New Caledonia was to train the Army Air Corps who were flying B-26s. We were to train them in torpedo warfare. They got there, but they didn't want to learn anything about torpedo warfare and they didn't want anything to do with us. I don't blame them. I suppose we showed them some approaches.

Once, while we were up in one of those B-26s, the pilot asked the gunnery officer what ammunition was loaded and the gunnery officer couldn't tell him. He didn't know. We were pretty amazed about that.

Our executive officer, Riley Hearst, was killed in an Army B-17. That left us three roving Navy boys at loose ends. We had a wonderful time for a couple of months. There was a campfire every night. No bombs. No worries.

We had raisins for breakfast and Spam for lunch and dinner. We were provisioned from a ship, and so sometimes we would get ham. We traded a ham to the Army for a Jeep. They were happy to have the ham, and we were happy to have the Jeep.

We were told that there may still be Japanese soldiers on the island. They equipped us with a Thompson submachine gun and a rifle, and we had our sidearms. We went to bed every night with all of those munitions, inside a mosquito net.

While in New Caledonia, Admiral John McCain's pilot checked me out on the admiral's PBY, his float plane. We were just fooling around I guess. The admiral never knew about that.

When we first got to New Caledonia, there was an OS2U sitting on a dock in a crate. The mechanics asked us if they could put it together. Only one of us, a pilot named Larry Steppenhagen, had been checked out on seaplanes. At Pensacola, there just weren't enough seaplanes for us to practice in. We asked him how to fly it, and he said, "You just hop in and push the throttle up." That was our preflight training in seaplanes.

A Tiger Moth, used for mail delivery at New Caledonia.

An OS2U Kingfisher

So they put it together, and we had a lot of fun with that. Another aircraft they had there was a British Tiger Moth bi-plane. I think it was a trainer. Everything was backward on it, and the fliers would always overcorrect on everything and make a mess of it.

We would fly the mail to the outposts on New Caledonia in that plane. We would just fly over and throw the mail over the side. Steppenhagen was flying the mail one day, and he flew into a tree. You can imagine what was left of the plane after that, and he ended up in the hospital.

It was my job to drive a Jeep from Noumea to Plan D'Gayak, a new airfield at the north end of the island, and pick up Steppenhagen. I didn't know the territory, and I didn't know if any Japs were along the way – either coast-watchers or left-behinders. I was a little nervous all the way.

Our sojourn in New Caledonia ended when we finally got a ship. It was an American passenger liner converted to a troop ship. We got on and headed for Sydney, Australia. On the way to Sydney we picked up some of the survivors of the action around Singapore. We brought them with us. They were British sailors, and some Indians. They were called Lascars, sailors from the southern India coast.

I had some 70 or 80 men under my charge. They were the old crewmen from our squadron. The other fellows gave me the delightful job of seeing the crewmen back to the United States while the other officers went directly back. It was a blessing for me. I got to Sydney, and got out to the Sydney Zoo and saw some of the weird animals, like a platypus, I'd heard about in college.

The ship remained at harbor for about a week, and every day I was free to go into Sydney and the zoo. We were assigned back to the United States on that troop ship, and we were blessed with cruise ship meals all the way back. There was a colonel, one of those impressed-with-his-rank fellows, and also an Army chaplain, and they were the only Army officers on board. The two of them just fought every time they saw each other all the way home. The trip home

New Caledonia was a territory of France located in the Coral Sea, part of Melonesia. The Coral Sea is due east of Australia in the southwest Pacific. The United States built a major naval base there at the beginning of the war, including a large repair facility at New Caledonia's major city, Noumea.

As the war moved north, New Caledonia became less and less important as a base. The Army's 23rd Infantry Division was stationed there and adopted the name the Americal Division, combining America and New Caledonia.

The torpedo bomber pilots on the USS Hornet. Only one survived the attack at the Battle of Midway. Sterrie always felt that the sinking of the Lexington, which prevented him from participating at Midway, may have saved his life. U.S. Navy photo.

>   The President of the United States takes pleasure in presenting the GOLD STAR in lieu of the Second Navy Cross to
>
>   LIEUTENANT NORMAN A. STERRIE
>   UNITED STATES NAVAL RESERVE
>
> for service as set forth in the following
>
>   CITATION:
>
>   "For extraordinary heroism and courageous devotion to duty as pilot of a torpedo plane in action against enemy forces in the Battle of the Coral Sea on May 8, 1942. In the face of heavy anti-aircraft fire and severe enemy fighter opposition, Lieutenant Sterrie closed to within a few hundred yards of his target to press home a fearless and determined attack and scored a hit upon an enemy Japanese aircraft carrier, thereby contributing to the severe damage and probable destruction of that vessel and aiding materially in the success attained by our forces."

Sterrie earned his second Navy Cross at the Battle of the Coral Sea.

took some 24 days. We were off the sea lanes, free from submarines. Finally we got back to the United States.

About those Torpedoes

I'm often asked about the performance of the American torpedoes. Before the war we used to have group exercises. I remember one in which torpedoes were involved. My experience that day, and the experience of others who participated, was that the torpedoes went every which way. I don't know if the torpedoes were better later on because I refused to carry them. I carried a 2,000-lb. bomb. You go in at 100 feet, and at about 200 feet from the ship, you let her go. Boom. This was my experience at Palau.

I once saw a story in a magazine that said our torpedoes had 6,000 intricate parts. No wonder they didn't work.

If the Lexington had not been sunk, it was probable that it would have been in the Battle of Midway. Of all the TBDs that flew that day at Midway, none of them came back. In fact, I'm the only pilot still alive who flew the TBD in combat. And there's not much of me left either.

Lt. Norman Sterrie is awarded the Distinguished Flying Cross for his actions in the attack on Palau in March of 1944. He earned the medal for destroying an enemy cargo ship and for the successful laying of mines in the Palau harbor.

Chapter Five
The New Lexington

Our squadron made it back to the U.S. We got orders to San Francisco and Torpedo Squadron 12, but when we arrived, there was no such thing that we could find.

I was ready to go on leave to Minnesota, but I didn't have a dress uniform. All my Navy clothes went down with the ship. All I had left were my khakis.

So I went down to the Walk Up a Flight and Save Ten store. I had gone to college with the son of the family that owned that company. The idea was that you climb to the second level, and you could get it cheaper. They were the only ones who could get me a uniform in time, so I could get on the train.

My old friends knew I was coming home, and when the train got to Butterfield, which is about 10 miles from St. James, my fellow band members from before boarded the train and rode with me into St. James. Then they escorted me off the train. There was a pa-

The second Lexington (CV-16) was the eighth carrier built in the Essex Class, and it was launched in February 1943. The new carrier was known as the Blue Ghost because of its distinctive coloring, and, also, like her predecessor, as the Lady Lex. The ship was 820 feet long and 147 feet wide. The ship displaced 36,000 tons with a full load of planes and gear.
The Lexington could cruise at 33 knots and was powered by eight boilers and four steam turbines. It was protected by its 110 aircraft and by 12 five-inch guns eight quadruple 40-millimeter guns, and 46 20-millimeter guns.
It carried a crew of 2,600.

The USS Lexington was launched in Boston Harbor on Feb. 17, 1943. The ship was originally to be named the Cabot, but the name was changed when the first Lexington was sunk at the Battle of the Coral Sea. Note the ice surrounding the ship and the snow on the flight deck. (U.S. Navy photo)

rade for the local hero returning. Betsy couldn't get off work in Minneapolis, so she couldn't be there. I was home for two weeks, and Betsy came back to San Francisco with me.

When I got back to San Francisco, I got orders to Torpedo 16, which was forming at Quonset Point, Rhode Island.

That was a long ways away. The speed limit at that time was 35 or 40 miles an hour, and I felt loyally committed to that. I requested extra time to drive across the country, and took the full two weeks. Betsy and I were in my little '39 Oldsmobile.

I had bought the car before the Lexington went to war, and I had a wreck the first night I bought it. I rear-ended someone in the rain. After I got it fixed, I was headed off to sea so I turned the little

Sterrie came home to St. James, after the first Lex was sunk, to a hero's welcome. The St. James newspaper proclaimed, "Sterries, a proud happy family." Norm is with his parents and sister Eloise at the train station. He is wearing his Walk Up a Flight and Save Ten uniform.

coupe over to my brother, who was working for one of the B-25 manufacturers on the coast. He hung onto it, insured it as it was, and he hoped for something bigger.

That car served us well all the way to the East Coast. We took the southern route all the way to mid-continent and then up to Quonset Point, arriving about Thanksgiving time of 1942.

I was assigned as executive officer to Robert Eisley with whom I'd served previously in Torpedo Squadron 2 in the early days. He was an Academy man. I think he picked me out. I also think that's why I was the only person in that whole air group who got sent right back out to sea.

Air Group 16 was assigned to the new Lexington,

The Grumman Avenger was the standard torpedo bomber for the Navy after the Battle of Midway, when many of the old Devastators were destroyed. It was designed by LeRoy Grumman, and the first batch was delivered to the fleet in 1942. The Avenger had a crew of three. It was 40 feet long, 54 feet wide, and was the heaviest single-engine plane the U.S. produced during the war. Its top speed was 276 miles per hour, and it had a range of 1,000 miles. It could carry a 2,000-pound torpedo or 2,000 pounds of bombs.

which was under construction at the Boston Navy Yard. It was originally destined to be named the Cabot, but, with the sinking of the first Lex, the name was changed.

I ended up doing all sorts of squadron organizational activities, including practice bombing, all out of the area around Boston and Quonset Point. It was a long winter for us up there, lots of snow. The runways had to be plowed, and landings were like going into a tunnel with high drifts on both sides.

Betsy and I lived on a nearby farm with a family. We had been staying in a room, but we met these people. They said there was no point in us just living in a room, and they asked us to join them as a family. So we did. And two dogs had dinner with us every night. Those two Rhode Islanders were very lovely people.

They launched Lexington in the spring of 1943. The air group went on the shakedown cruise on the new ship, and we got as far as Norfolk. It turned out the aviation gasoline tanks were leaking, and that smell permeated the whole ship. The smoking lamp was out – no smoking – for the entire ship until we could land. We were sitting on a potential explosion all the time. We were probably in Norfolk for a week's time until that was repaired.

Comparing the new Lex with the old Lex, I would say that carriers are about the same. The landings are about the same. The procedures were all the same. From that standpoint I don't think there was much difference. The ship was a bit shorter than the old Lex. The first one had been a modification of a battle cruiser, and I believe it was the longest carrier of its time. The second one was in the Essex class of carriers and maybe a hundred feet shorter.

The new one had a lot more cabins. For the first time we had our own ready room, which was a wonderful place for predawn gatherings as well as night briefings. To have your own ready room was really kind of a luxury. It was just off the group commander's cabin.

I was flying the Avenger, which was the Navy's new torpedo bomber. We had two .50-caliber guns, one on each wing. They were fixed. What did we use the guns for? That's a good question. We wondered why we even had them in those planes. I suppose they wanted to improve on the .30-caliber single guns on the first TBD. We never strafed. We never fired at an enemy aircraft. We never had the occasion to use them.

I did love the Avenger, though. It went 190 miles an hour compared with the 90 miles an hour in the Devastator. I was very excited. It was really fast.

On our way south, on July 24, 1943, I flew the intelligence officer into Guantanamo Bay to get information on submarines in the area. So I could always say that I landed at Guantanamo. I just landed and took off; didn't have a chance to visit.

The rest of the shakedown cruise that August was to the Gulf of Paria, just north of Venezuela where there's a harbor. It was a place at sea that could actually be walled off from the submarines.

It was at Paria that we lost Nile Kinnick, the former University of Iowa quarterback and Heisman Trophy winner. He was a fighter pilot, and his plane developed an oil leak, and he had to land in

Sterrie, center, stood in front of an Avenger with two other pilots from the Lexington.

the water some distance from the Lex. They never found his body. Iowa's Kinnick Stadium is named after him.

I had reported to Quonset in late November, and by late August we were on our way to the Pacific. The Essex Class carriers could go through the Panama Canal, but first they had to take the side-mount guns off so it would clear. They put them on again on the other side. It was pretty tight, but

The Battle of Tarawa in the Gilbert Islands was fought in late November 1943, and it was the second major offensive in the Pacific.
The U.S. needed to secure land bases for its bombers in order to attack Japanese bases in the Marianas.
About 35,000 Marines and Army soldiers landed on Nov. 20 and the next two days. A force of about 4,000 Japanese defended the island.
In the 72-hour battle, the U.S. lost nearly 1,700 killed while more than 2,100 were wounded. Nearly the entire Japanese force was killed.

Sterrie received his first Air Medal for the missions at Tarawa in 1943. "Sterrie pressed home his attacks skillfully and with agressive determination in the face of intense, persistent anti-aircraft fire, accurately placing his bombs on the as-signed targets and inflicting heavy damage on the enemy."

we squeezed through. We were on our way then to the Hawaiian Islands.

As we neared Pearl Harbor, we were ordered to stage a combat exercise as a squadron. We were to make a combat attack, which we did, much to the dismay of our squadron and the Navy in general. There was a mid-air collision on the part of two of our aircraft on the way in. The planes crashed to the earth, and I think some 19 people were killed in a machine shop in one of the areas at Pearl.

Three of our crew didn't make it, and three survived that crash. I guess one of the planes wasn't damaged enough to prevent them from bailing out. Norm White, the pilot of the other torpedo bomber, was killed. The Avenger had three-man crews comprised of the pilot, the radioman and radar man, and the gunner.

It was very sad to lose a friend, but it was the first of many more. We had lost one pilot on the first Lex in the Coral Sea action. He ran out of fuel on the way back to the carrier. A destroyer was sent to the area, but there was no sign of anything.

First Mission

We made a preliminary attack on Tarawa on September 18. It was to be our first mission, and whoever decided the takeoff time must have been a little bit off because the takeoff was at night, and we reached the target in the night. It was difficult to see anything.

We were just attacking the island in general. We had no fixed targets. Nobody could distinguish anything down there. We made two raids that night.

The rendezvous on the way to the target at Tarawa was a joke. There was no order whatsoever. Everybody joined up on any other plane he could find and went in as sections, perhaps two planes at a time, strung out from the carrier to the target. As we reached the target, the outline was apparent by starlight. The tracers against the first planes soon appeared.

Officers and men aboard the Lexington keep track of the progress of the attack on Tarawa. (U.S. Navy photo)

One by one, people made their dives. Before they went in, they yelled, "I'm going in now." And everybody else stayed clear. There was one big explosion on the island, a fuel dump probably.

We returned to the ship, and it was decided right there that we needed more practice on making a rendezvous. We went back to Naval Air Station Kaneohe Bay in Hawaii, and the group was stationed there for a while.

We were involved at Wake Island, which was the next thing after Tarawa. Wake was in enemy hands when we made an attack, this time carrying torpedoes. Without any advanced information about what was there, the Navy had us carry these torpedoes. It was just a waste of energy. There

Lt. "Bud" Deering, the Landing Signal Officer on the Lexington, brings a plane aboard during the operations in the Gilbert Islands in November 1943. (U.S. Navy photo)

was one ship in the harbor, and the harbor was so shallow that the torpedoes certainly hit the bottom anyway.

An interesting thing about Wake was that one pilot was shot down, and was saved by his crewman. He had bumped his head when he crashed, and the crewman got him into the lifeboat. In the meantime, this pilot's section leader was flying on top, and he broadcast that these men were in the lifeboat. He asked that they please send a destroyer out to recover them. He repeated it a few minutes later. And furthermore, he told the command that he would only go back to the ship after he saw a destroyer come to pick up his fellow pilot.

I talked to the downed pilot after the war, and he said it was quite an experience. There was a submarine in the area, and night was falling. He would flash his little light, and the submarine raised the conning tower and flashed a light. He was drifting into shore, which would have been lethal. Fortunately, the submarine managed to pick him up. His name was Padilla.

A few days later, all the pilots were ordered to report to the ready room and thereupon were given a lecture by the admiral. Bradford Grow was his name. He announced that we're at war now, and when you get a command, you carry it out. There would be no more foolishness such as asking destroyers to come out and do a rescue. To his credit, the admiral went back to Washington, and on all our subsequent missions, the target was surrounded by at least three submarines. We knew their positions, so we could glide in to get help if we were shot down. An Avenger will float five to 10 minutes at the most.

Depending upon the circumstances, you always have that choice of whether to try and land the plane or bail out. If you know where the sub is, and you can glide to it, you just land in the water. I don't know what that's like because I never had to do it. Two of my pilots at Saipan had to do it, and one of the fellows who was shot down at Saipan, at the Philippine Sea action, was shot down again and was recovered both times. We felt better about making attacks when we had the submarines around.

No More Torpedoes

After Wake, I refused to carry those torpedoes anymore. Often we didn't know what the target was and if they'd be the best weapon. And, there were the tremendous risks in trying to get in close enough to drop them. It was more foolishness – to risk your life over nothing.

The whole squadron carried bombs. We chose the munitions we would carry. I usually elected to carry four 500-pound bombs, rather than a 2,000-pound bomb, which would have been more effective, but you'd have less of a chance of hitting anything. We could also carry two 1,000-pound bombs, but again with less chance of a hit. The more-is-better theory seemed to work when one of

Planes are recovered on the Lex in November 1943. (U.S. Navy photo)

Mili Atoll (sometimes spelled "Mille") is in the Marshall Islands and had been occupied by the Japanese since 1914. An airstrip had been built across the island.

The island was taken by U.S. forces in 1944.

my pilots dropped his four bombs on a carrier, and they all hit. His crewman watched them hit.

When we carried the four bombs, we were doing glide bombing. It's about halfway between dive bombing and masthead bombing. Dive bombing is where you come straight down at the target. Masthead bombing is where you come in right over the water and drop the bomb before you go by. In glide bombing, you come in at about a 60 degree angle and drop from about 2,000 feet.

Sterrie's aviator's flight logbook for November 1943. The early flights were from the Naval Air Station at Kaneohe, Hawaii. The columns record various bits of information about the flight. For example, on November 9, Sterrie flew a TBF Avenger, plane number 24429, on a cross country flight that took about 35 minutes. He was accompanied by his radioman and his gunner, Patschke and Klingbeil. On November 19 and 22, he flew missions to Mili. Sterrie indicates the number of the carrier landing (C/L). On November 22, he made his 244th carrier landing. Sterrie lost his original logbook when the first Lex was sunk.

I think there was one squadron at Saipan that still used torpedoes. I don't know how they fared. If the enemy anti-aircraft fire was diverted by the dive bombers, maybe you might make it. But if you go in all alone, you take your chances.

This led up to the next mission, which was at Mili Atoll in the Marshall Islands to the north. Tarawa was about to be attacked by the Marines, and our mission as torpedo planes and perhaps the whole air group was to protect the Marines from any attack from the north. In all likelihood, it would have been from Mili.

As we took off for the attack on Mili, on the way up, we encountered a major atmospheric front, which meant we had to fly through as an air group in formation for about 10 to 20 minutes on instruments. We had never done that before. There was no buffeting of the plane, but we simply couldn't see where we were going. You had to keep track of your distance by radar, and I was probably the only plane in that group that had radar. You try to regroup when you come out the other side. There was no point in communicating because all attention was on the instruments – flying.

I was on the tail end of things with my six planes. I entered in a wide turn, which must have been confusing to one of the pilots, because he never showed up when we came out in the clear.

We never saw him again. He just disappeared. We surmised that he got into a deadly circle in which you look like you're on an even keel with the horizontal instruments, but actually you're winding up tighter and tighter and you finally go in.

What happens is that you're increasing in speed and tightening your turn, so your control stick is deep into your lap, and you can go no tighter. Finally, the turn is so tight that you lose the speed necessary to keep airborne. It's a trap that people on instruments can get into. Fortunately it only happened to one of us. He was a pilot with lesser capabilities, and we had debated whether to take him along or not on the cruise.

That pilot was the first I'd lost under my direct command. I felt bad about it, of course. But such is war. As I said, there were many more to follow.

It's fairly obvious to the other pilots whether a pilot is up to par. There are skills – joining up in rendezvous for instance, or performance in the accuracy of his bombing efficiency – that you can judge another pilot by.

We got up to Mili on November 19, and the group made the attack. We encountered no air opposition. We went after anything that looked alive down there. I was the executive officer of the torpedo squadron, which meant that I had half the squadron flying under me.

Mili had a large Japanese airstrip, and it was a favorite target of American warplanes. It was kind of a practice area, but not without its dangers because one of our squadron commanders made a low pass, and his plane was pretty well shot up. He managed to keep aloft anyway and make it back.

While you were on any mission, it was serious business, but I think there was a sense of lightness

Commander Paul Buie briefs his fighter pilots of VF-16 about the next mission during November or December 1943. Buie was the fighter squadron leader. (U.S. Navy photo)

after you got back. You were glad to be alive. Of course, in your mind, you had to review every step of the way.

The Battle for Tarawa was now underway. It was a very costly battle. There was a favorite Marine writer, Bob Sherrod, who came aboard the Lexington for a time. His claim to fame was his writing about the Battle of Tarawa. He went ashore when it was not under complete control of our forces. He wrote of being pinned down by enemy fire behind a pier of some kind. We liked him because he spent more time with the men than the brass above decks.

I was in contact with him after the war, just before he died from the effects of cigarettes. He was a cigarette-after-cigarette man. He was an editor of Time Magazine during the war, and he later was editor of the Saturday Evening Post.

He interviewed me, and I have a copy of the transcript. He told a friend of mine, who happened to be traveling with that Time-Life business, that he could prove he was with me because he had a copy of our conversations. He gave it to this friend, who gave it to me. I have it in my stuff somewhere. I think the interview was in the book on the capture of Tarawa.

We didn't talk to journalists very often. I think the pilots were pleased to talk to anybody who asked, but there weren't many journalists on board. We had on the Lexington at one time the famous photographer Edward Steichen, who was named a commander by the Navy. I have a picture from the Guggenheim Museum that he shot, where I'm watching a recovery. Another Steichen photo showed our fighter squadron celebrating after the attack on Mili. He also took some pictures of the fueling operation, which was really something to watch. That operation was a lengthy one for the carrier.

While we were at sea, everybody's mail had to be censored. The officers censored the crew, and the officers also censored each other. We did it with a pen. I don't think we censored very much. The Japanese knew all the things we talked about anyway. We listened to Tokyo Rose. She reported the Lexington sunk a number of times.

After Mili, in early December, was Kwajalein. The ship was under attack from early morning. We were awakened by gunfire – not the usual reveille. The mission was supposed to be a surprise, but the surprise was on us. The pilots were told to "man your planes," and we grabbed a chart board or whatever and our vests and hopped in the plane. As the ship was turning around into the wind, all the planes were loaded and ready to go. My engine was turned up, and I was ready to take off. I looked up, and here was this bomb going over my head. It was maybe 10 feet over my head, and then I saw the bottom of an airplane just ahead of it. He hung on to it one or two seconds too long, and it went over the ship and dropped in the water. I think I said, "Oh, shit."

If that bomb had hit those planes, that Japanese pilot would have been a hero to his people – all those planes, all that gasoline, all those bombs.

Later that day, the ship was hit by a torpedo. I was

Kwajalein Atoll in the Marshall Islands, about 2,100 miles from Hawaii, was the site of another costly American landing as the U.S. moved across the Pacific. There were 8,000 Japanese defenders on the island, and nearly all of them were killed. The U.S. landed two divisions of 42,000 men on the various islets, and about 400 were killed. The battle lasted from the end of January to the beginning of February 1944.

The USS Lexington launched a raid on Kwajalein Atoll on December 4, 1943, as part of the softening-up of the island prior to the U.S. invasion which would come two months later.
The morning strike destroyed a large Japanese cargo ship and damaged two destroyers. However, the Japanese learned the position of the Lexington and launched a night attack. At 11:32 that night, a Japanese torpedo hit the Lex on the starboard side, knocking out her steering and killing nine men. The ship began listing and circling in a dense cloud of smoke caused by the explosion. Temporary repairs were made, and by December 9 the ship made it to Pearl Harbor, where the air squadrons were put ashore. By February 20, the ship was in drydock in Bremerton, Wash.
Lexington didn't return to duty until March 1944.

Sterrie earned an Air Medal at Mili and Kwajalein in November and December, 1943.

The citation, signed by Secretary of the Navy James Forrestal, said:

"Undaunted by intense antiaircraft fire encountered during this period, Lieutenant Commander (then Lieutenant) Sterrie boldly led three damaging bombing attacks against hostile installations at Mili and launched a close range torpedo attack at Kwajalein where he inflected heavy damage on a light enemy cruiser. By his leadership, skill as an airman and courageous devotion to duty, Lieutenant Commander Sterrie contributed materially to the success of his squadron. His conduct throughout upheld the highest traditions of the Naval Service."

Chronologically, this was Sterrie's second Air Medal, but it was listed in naval records as his third. His second Air Medal, according to the Navy, was at Hollandia and New Guinea in March 1944.

just stepping through a hatch when I felt a tremendous hit. I had no doubt about what had happened. The ship got hit in the rudder, and, at that particular time, we were in a sharp turn. We stayed in a sharp turn for about an hour under a full moon. The rest of the fleet shoved off and left us with one destroyer to guard us. Fortunately, the Japs never came back, or we'd have really been in trouble.

That torpedo put us out of commission for a few months. We had to steer using our screws, and we headed back to Hawaii.

One day after we arrived, we were at the officer's club in Hawaii and enjoying a few refreshments. The squadron skipper had been sent back to the States, and I was in charge of the torpedo squadron. A message arrived at the club. They wanted us to supply two pilots for target practice until midnight. That was a problem. Who was sober? Luckily we had a couple of pilots who didn't drink, and they volunteered.

The ship then went to Bremerton, Washington, for major repairs. We kept busy, but I didn't have another carrier landing until March, 1944, when the Lexington returned.

AIRPLANE ON FIRE

During my time overseas, I came close to ditching my plane once.

I think the ship was going to Palau. It was in early March 1944. The torpedo bunch took off and we were circling around, and we were going to test our guns. We were probably at about 3,000 feet. I fired my guns, and a fire broke out in a compartment in the left wing. A cartridge blew up and severed a hydraulic line and started a fire in the outer part of the wing.

The aileron was on fire, and there was a huge flame licking at the tail of the ship. I thought I'd better get my crew out. They may have to jump, and I might not have time to warn them to get out. I told them to get out, and I was preparing to jump myself. I had

The Grumman TBF Avenger was the replacement for the slow Douglas TBD Devastators used in the first part of the war. Sterrie began flying the new planes when he came back to the United States after the sinking of the first Lexington. (U.S. Navy photo)

one foot on the wing and one foot in the cockpit, going about 140 knots. As I was about to jump, I looked over at the fire, which seemed to be going out.

I kept on flying without using any of the controls. As long as it was flying in a straight line, that was good enough. The crew was picked up by a fishing boat down below, I found out later.

Now I had to land this sucker. I was in the air and doing well and I spied an island ahead with an airstrip. I kept her at level flight and descended to the runway. It was a fairly new runway designed to handle much larger planes. It was fortunate that it was long.

It turned out to be Majuro, the new western base for the Navy. The horizontal and vertical stabilizers were untouched; it was just the aileron on the left wing that was damaged. I would not have risked a carrier landing, and I don't think they would have wanted to take me aboard, at least not while I was on fire.

I descended, and, of course, I had no flaps. I also didn't know if I had wheels down or not; I had no one to tell me. I feared shaking the plane to get the wheels down might raise some trouble with the structure of the wing. So I just descended and tried to make my landing at about 140 knots. Our usual landing speed was about 60.

As I came down, there was a Marine plane taking up the first 100 yards of the runway. His engine had cut off, and he was in trouble. The crew was hopping on that plane to see what was wrong. I had to clear that one, and not knowing if the wheels were down or not, I let the plane down as easily as possible. The wheels touched. They were down.

I used up most of that runway, but finally came to a stop. I hurriedly jumped out of the plane. The wing was still smoking, and it was very near one of the gasoline tanks. Somebody picked me up in a Jeep and took me into operations. I inquired as to whether they had any extra planes that I could take back to the ship. They told me the Yorktown had left two planes, but they didn't know what condition they were in. I was welcome to take one of those.

I hurriedly went out to one of them, turned it up, started it, and it seemed to be working all right. So, I took off, heading for the ship, which was on its way to Palau. It was 30 to 40 miles out by that time. They made room for me on the ship, and I landed the plane on the carrier.

All was well, I thought, and I at least had one plane for the next operation. The next day the engineering officer approached me and said, "Why didn't you stay where you were? We had to change the engine on that plane overnight."

PALAU

At the end of March 1944, we learned there was an assembly of Japanese ships in the harbor at Palau, and we were going to attack them. I flew that mission with another flight crew, other than the crew I was used to, but it all worked well. I had the job of mining the harbor. Well, I had half the job, with six of my planes to mine the north half of the harbor. One of the small carriers mined the other entrance to the harbor. These were aerial mines. You could only carry one mine per flight.

We had a man who came specially from Washington to talk to us about the mines. To place the mines correctly meant finding a checkpoint on land and flying so many seconds and dropping the mine. It meant flying straight and level, and we never like to do that where there's opposition. We'd have to go so many seconds, and each plane was flying a different number of seconds before they dropped.

That was the first mission of the day. The rest of the group that wasn't laying mines had a field day with the enemy ships. No opposition. There were 30 or more ships in the harbor, and they cleaned them up.

Sterrie receives an Air Medal, probably his first, during a Navy ceremony.

Palau was another step in the U.S. war strategy of island hopping toward the Japanese homeland.

Located 500 miles east of the Philippines and 2,000 miles south of Tokyo, the series of islands had been controlled by Japan since 1914.

The Marines landed on Peleliu, one of the islands in the group, in September 1944, and later an Army division also landed.

The battle for Peleliu had the highest U.S. casualty rate of any island assault in the war.

The attacks from the Lexington in March 1944 helped prepare the island for invasion some months later.

On the second mission of the day, there was very little left, but I spotted a good sized ship that I chose as my target. I attacked out of the sun, approached at top speed, close to 300 knots, and pulled out of my dive at about 100 feet. I flew into this ship and let a 2,000-pound bomb go. There was no more ship.

This was not free of trouble, though, because my wingman got shot down. I worried for a while that my wingman might have encountered the debris falling from the sky from my bomb. But, later, other pilots told me he was hit by anti-aircraft fire.

He brought his plane down, or maybe the plane went down by itself on one of the coral reefs outside the harbor. It crashed, and the gunner in that plane, we figured later, had to escape through the turret, which must have been jarred loose during the crash. He got out of the turret and was on the coral reef when the rescue submarine sent out a small life boat to get the crew. They were under fire from a shore battery, but they made it back to the submarine OK. Later the crew and this gunner made it back to our carrier.

Sterrie earned the Distinguished Flying Cross for his work at Palau. The citation, signed by Admiral Chester Nimitz, read, in part: "He fearlessly and accurately delivered a masthead bombing attack upon a cargo vessel with all his bombs scoring hits. Immediately following his attack the vessel exploded and sank. These tasks were accomplished despite determined opposition by the enemy in the form of intense anti-aircraft fire."
The photo of Sterrie receiving his medal leads off this chapter.

The Navy awarded Sterrie his third Air Medal, officially recorded as his second, at Hollandia. It cited his "aggressive and determined" action.

The citation said, "By his expert airmanship, indomitable fighting spirit, inspiring leadership and cool courage in the face of terrific opposition, Lieutenant Commander Sterrie contributed materially to the success of his squadron..."

He was the only man in my command who asked not to fly again. I couldn't blame him. I said, "You won't fly again under my command." He had been through enough in my book.

He said he was afraid to fly, not in so many words, but in what he told me. It was a terrible experience, to be shot down and then crash afterward.

At the end of that day at Palau, there was one ship remaining and that was a hospital ship. We had plenty of planes to do it in, but nobody attacked it. That was our policy.

As for the other targets, you don't worry about killing people. There are too many of the enemy after you.

Somewhere in there, I think we also hit a place called Woleai. That's the only mission I don't remember making.

HOLLANDIA AND TRUK

We went to support Gen. Douglas MacArthur's operation in April 1944. We went to Hollandia, New Guinea. I had the job of ferrying one of the ship's officers who had been detached. I had to take him over to Admiralty Island. So, I missed some of the show at Hollandia. I flew three missions, but whatever was there was emptied out. I think the group just dropped bombs on an airfield there. One of the pilots dared to make a touch and go landing on the airstrip there. It was foolishness. He had a kind a clown ship's officer in the back seat, and I think he had a dare to do that. There was no opposition at that place.

The next mission I remember was Truk which we hit on the way back to be replenished.

Truk had been the major Japanese base before the war, but now had been reduced to an outpost. We made an attack on Truk and what I remember most about it, we had to carry rockets. The rockets were really placed a lot of drag on the airplane, and we never had a chance to practice with them. We just pressed the trigger, and off they went. We didn't know where

The USS Lexington cuts a large wake as it recovers a plane in the Pacific. (U.S. Navy photo)

they were going, except they were going the direction of the plane.

I saw a small ship in the harbor, and made my rocket attack on it, but I wasn't very satisfied with that mission. One of my pilots at that time was a fellow named Swanson. He was a Minneapolis boy, too. He was later killed after the war in that mystic Bermuda Triangle off the East Coast.

On this mission, Swanson took a hit in his engine, and it was belching out oil and smoke. I asked him to join up on me and I'd get him back. He joined up, and we got back to the ship. He was able to make a carrier landing with that engine. It had at least two cylinders less than what it started with. It must have been a rough road for him on the way home.

Sterrie posed for this portrait after he had been promoted to Lieutenant Commander.

Lt. Cmdr. Edward Steichen, a well-known photographer before the war, was assigned for a time to the USS Lexington. This Steichen photograph of a launch appeared in Life Magazine. In the upper left of the photo, three naval officers are watching the launch. Sterrie is on the right. (U.S. Navy photo)

Chapter Six
Philippine Sea

It was June 1944, and we were covering the landings at Saipan. Torpedo 16 initially was covering the area to the north, and there were several islands that we were making sure had no activity coming from them. On one of the initial attacks on Saipan, my commanding officer, Bob Isely, was ordered to take out one corner of an airfield's gun emplacements and I had the other corner. Isely was using rockets, and it didn't work well.

In his initial dive, Isely was shot down and killed. That left me as squadron commander. Also lost on that mission was Ensign Delgado, who flew in right behind Isely. Delgado was killed while he was parachuting down.

I was in the second group to take off, and I learned that Bob had been killed and that we'd lost another man. We made our dive and returned to the ship to re-arm.

You have heard of the Lexington
And the Yorktown's Gallant Crew
They're the fightin', flyin' men
Who wear the Navy blue.

And where these men have shown the way
These and many more.
There'll always be a fighting man
To even up the score!

An excerpt from the poem "Flight Quarters" by Robert H. Isely, Commander of Torpedo 16, who was killed while attacking an airfield in the invasion of Saipan. Sterrie took over as the CO of the squadron. The airfield on Saipan was later renamed after Isely.

In his scrapbooks, Sterrie has a collection of aerial photos of Saipan, used by the pilots to plan their attack. Sterrie's skipper, Robert Isely, was killed attacking this airfield.

Bob Isely and I had served together in VT-2 aboard the old Lex, and that's why I think I got involved so much in the war. I was the only person to go back the second time. I think it was because he asked for me.

Paul Dana was in Isely's crew and was also killed. I think he was of the New York newspapering family.

On the next mission, I had excellent communications with the ground forces, and we were directed by the color of the bomb bursts where they wanted us to drop our bombs. It's interesting that just recently I was at a luncheon for the Saipan survivors, and I told them that I was covering from on top, taking instructions from below, and out of the crowd came a voice that said, "I was on the other end of that

Sailors watch the contrails of the planes during the Turkey Shoot. (U.S. Navy photo)

In one of the most famous pictures of World War II, Alex Vraciu holds up six fingers to indicate how many Japanese planes he shot down in the Marianas Turkey Shoot. Vraciu was one of Sterrie's fellow pilots aboard the Lexington, and by the end of the war was the Navy's fourth leading fighter ace with 19 kills. (U.S. Navy photo)

communication. I was telling you where to drop the bombs." This was years after the war.

There was a problem at Saipan with the direction of the attack. If you came at it from the direction where the troops were at, you might risk the possibility of an early drop, so you had to plan your approach in the perpendicular direction. (Sterrie indicated with his hands the plan of attack.) The bursts were here, we were circling over here, our troops were here. We'd come in from the side. The Marines were trained in this and we were not.

The Japanese were responding to the battle for Saipan with all their energies. There was a collection of Japanese carriers and support ships to the west of us, out of our range, but within theirs. Their planes were certainly able to fly a longer range than ours.

So, even though we knew they were massing a big armada to the west of us, we could do nothing about it. We knew that they would strike sooner or later, and the orders to our torpedo planes were to clear the decks. This was going to be a fighter operation, no matter what. We should clear the decks and remain within a few miles of our carriers. All of our ships were in the air, and the decks

Taken from the book *Mission Beyond Darkness* by Lt. Cdr. J. Bryan and Philip Reed Duell, Sloan and Pearce, NY, 1945

When the scout planes finally located the Japanese fleet on June 20, 1944, at 4:24 in the afternoon, Vice Admiral Marc Mitscher had a tough decision to make. To send out his planes would mean that many of them might not have enough fuel to get back, and all of them would have to land in the dark.

"Launch 'em!" Mitscher ordered.

When it came time to launch the Avengers from the Lexington, they took off in this order: Tom Bronn, Warren McLellan, Kent Cushman, Clint Swanson, Bill Linn, Buzzie Thomas and Norm Sterrie. Linn's plane developed an oil leak, so he jettisoned its bombs and returned to land on another carrier.

"Sterrie was the most experienced pilot in the squadron, and one of the most daring," said author Bryan.

Sterrie led one section with Swanson on his left and Bronn on his right. Cushman led the other section with McLellan on his left and Thomas on his right.

After the first launch, Mitscher decided against launching the rest of the planes.

As the American planes headed were cleared for the fighters only. We could fly for three or four hours.

The order came: They're on their way. Our scouts discovered them taking off. I remember this was a Sunday. We carried our chart boards with us wherever we went in case the order came and we had to run for the planes. We'd have to take off without any further instructions.

They sent some 400 planes in, and this was the Great Turkey Shoot, as defined by Paul Buie at a later time. None of their planes got through. Up to 400 got launched, and everything either got shot down or was dispersed to other airfields in the area on Tinian, Guam. The torpedo bombers and the dive bombers just circled off to the side. We listened to the traffic on the radio.

The Japanese leaders never realized what had happened. The failed return of their planes was accepted as a fact of probably landing at other fields in the area. The next day, we knew there would be further trouble, and the decision was made after the position report came in that we would take off with suitable armament to go after them. They were on their way back to Japan.

Word came in rather late in the day that the Japanese fleet was spotted. The admiral decided to send half of our planes after them. I took off with six planes, and the other squadrons divided accordingly. The Japanese carriers were at the limits of our range, but we took off in pursuit.

About halfway to the target we received a new position report for the Japanese fleet, which was now 60 to 70 miles farther away than was originally given. This presented a real problem for us. But we were loaded with bombs and ready for action. We continued on to the target.

As we approached the target, the anti-aircraft bursts were apparent overhead. As I rounded a huge cloud in preparation for getting away from our dive bombers for a coordinated attack, we were hit by Zeros. One of the planes in my group was shot down

Admiral Marc Mitscher is shown on the bridge of the Lexington during the Battle of the Philippine Sea. Mitscher launched his planes, knowing they might not have enough fuel to get back, but he left the lights on for them when they did return. (Life Magazine photo)

– McLellan along with his crew, Hutchinson and Selby.

In any mission, your best chance of a hit would be if the ship is coming at you and at about 30 degrees. Hitting the target broadside is the worst because you have the least to aim at. You'd maneuver in the air to line up the target. But at Saipan, as I rounded this huge cloud and then spotted them down below, the Japanese carrier had just come out of a turn and was set up for me. If it hadn't been that way, I would have tried for a better angle. You don't fly 250 miles and then throw away something for nothing.

So, there below me was the enemy fleet. I pushed over to enter my glide, and in the middle of the glide, due west to find the Japanese fleet, they got a radio message that told them that the enemy fleet was 70 miles farther than they had been first told.

The Japanese fleet was first spotted at 6:23 p.m. and by 6:45 it could be seen that there were three groups of Japanese ships. Lt. Cmdr. Ralph Weymouth was in charge of the Lexington's bombers. Sterrie heard over his headphones, "No enemy planes in the air over target." Minutes later two Japanese "Zekes" or Zeros attacked the torpedo bombers and McLellan was hit. In the movement to get ready for the attack, somehow the fighters and bombers became separated, and there was no fighter support during the bombing.

The anti-aircraft fire was terrible for the pilots. "In the dusk below, the ships seemed to be ablaze, so incessantly did the gun muzzles flash and twinkle. And, in the sunlight above, the bursts formed a solid roof."

The Lexington's planes attacked the Japanese group which contained two Hayataka-class carriers. At 7:04 p.m., the dive bombers went in. They dropped 14 1,000-pound bombs and got seven hits on one carrier and one hit on the other.

The TBMs were carrying four 500-pound armor-piercing bombs each. The Avengers went "over the top" at 9,500 feet and at 7,000 feet opened the bay doors. At 3,000 feet, Sterrie released, hitting the carrier with one bomb and probably another, according to Byran. Bronn hit the flattop with all four bombs. In all, nine bombs hit the carrier.

The Avengers skimmed above the water at about 50 feet, avoiding some of the anti-aircraft fire, and passed between two Japanese destroyers. Four Zeros dove down at Sterrie and Swanson. One attacked Sterrie's plane from dead astern, and gunner Jack Webb put 40 rounds into its belly and then watched as it crashed and burned.

Sterrie had the chart board on his lap, trying to figure out the route home.

Sterrie said, "Look, boys, we're going to get home. Cut the chatter and shoot the best you can." Just then two more Zekes came roaring at the Avengers. "Oh, Lord," Sterrie said.

By this time, the attackers were getting some cover from the missing fighters. About 50 planes from several carriers had gathered up, and the pilots were sticking their fingers through the holes in their canopies to show where they'd been hit. At 7:18 p.m., 14 minutes since the attack began, the air group settled in on a course of 100 degrees.

Cushman drew up beside Sterrie and held up six fingers, and

probably halfway down from the nearly 10 thousand or 12 thousand feet, now down to six or eight, an anti-aircraft burst exploded right off my nose, maybe 50 yards ahead, straight on.

Poof. It was enough to make me jump. There's no shock in the air. Even if there's a lot of anti-aircraft around you, there's no turbulence, just a black puff.

That one might have been the closest in all my attacks, but I don't know. It was 35 missions, you know, and that's a lot of being shot at.

In the jolt of that near miss, my thumb was on the trigger, releasing my bombs. Fortunately, I was on target. McLellan, in his parachute, halfway down, observed that two of my bombs had hit the carrier.

As I descended to deck level, now circling, waiting for the others to join up, I heard and felt the chatter of my guns. I looked back and saw a Japanese fighter headed for the water. My gunner had shot him down.

I stayed low so that the other planes could see me and join up in a hurry. You tried to make yourself the least effective target. Most likely you continued with your nose down and the faster the better.

Now begins some real trouble. It's getting pretty late, the sun is low on the horizon. We're 250 miles from nowhere, with all that distance to go and not knowing if we had enough fuel to get us there. I ordered my flight to fly in a loose formation and not jockey their throttles all the time so that they could observe a pattern of saving their fuel.

If you're using the least amount of fuel possible, you can observe practically no emission from the exhaust, or at best a blue flame signifying that everything put in had been consumed. You just wanted the engine turning over enough to keep yourself airborne at a reasonably safe speed.

This was going to be a difficult proposition, for we were going to have about 175 planes – 25 having been shot down over the target – arriving at the same time – at night – all short of fuel.

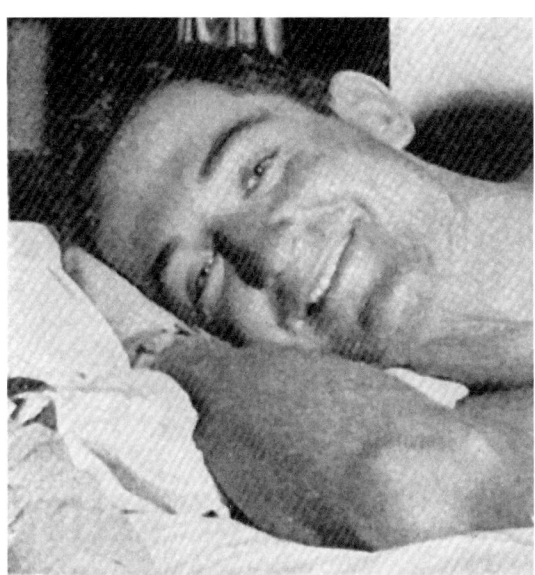

June 21. This morning a destroyer picked up a pilot named Warren E. McLellan whose experience was certainly one of the strangest as well as one of the most valuable of the whole war. Piloting one of our torpedo bombers, McLellan found his plane, hit by Japanese antiaircraft fire, on fire about 5,000 feet above the target. He and his crewmen bailed out and floated down safely through the hail of fire, presumably because the Japanese gunners were too busy with our planes to bother with them. McLellan hit the water in the midst of the enemy fleet. From this point of vantage he was in a position to ascertain exactly what damage our bombers had done. McLellan and his crewmen watched Japanese rescue boats scour the sea by searchlight for survivors. When the fleet moved on he was attacked by sharks which he clubbed with his shoes. Today a search plane dropped him a raft, and finally, 14 hours after his jump, a destroyer picked him up. McLellan's story, as told to Admiral Mitscher, would certainly in terms of journalism justify several dozen Pulitzer prizes. Its military significance was that he had seen one Japanese carrier blow up and two others burning brightly, listing badly and apparently about to sink. After delivering it, in quiet monosyllables prompted by sympathetic questions from Mitscher, McLellan seemed a little weary and the ship's surgeon sent him down to sick bay.

Lieut. (j.g.) Warren Mc Lellan parachuted from burning torpedo plane in middle of enemy task force, saw entire battle was rescued after 14 hours in the water

In a July 1944 issue of Life Magazine, a longer story about the attack on Saipan featured an item on Warren McLellan, who was shot down while attacking the Japanese fleet.

As we approached the fleet, we had no trouble finding it because the admiral had ordered all the lights on on every ship. There were lights up into the air. We had a very direct route once we neared them. As we approached our formation, there was pandemonium, desperate cries. There were pilots trying to land on the same ship at the same time.

In fact, there were three large carriers out of commission at the same time with deck crashes due to inexperienced pilots making carrier landings at night. I freed my crew to do as they saw fit, and I went up top for a while. I had a feeling that one more plane in this mess was not going to do any good.

After things had quieted down, I had another 15 minutes of air time remaining in my fuel tank. You fly on all the reserve tanks first, so you have a final say on

then one, to indicate that plane 61 had been shot down. Sterrie checked his knee pad and found out it was McLellan. "Sterrie looked up again, shaking his head slowly."

In all, 33 planes had launched from the Lexington. The long flight home began with 27 planes.

On the way back, the group formed up with the five TBMs in the center, led by Sterrie, flying in a compact group. On the port side was Bombing 16 and a few scattered strangers. On the starboard side were planes

One of the carriers attacked by the Lexington's planes on June 20, 1944, was the Japanese carrier Zuikaku, shown here in a sweeping curve with bombs exploding all around her. Zuikaku was severely damaged in the attack, but managed to return to port.

from several carriers including SBDs, TBMs, F6Fs and SB2Cs.

At first the group followed Weymouth's lead, but Sterrie had plotted his own course and determined that Weymouth was about five degrees off. Sterrie and his group went their own way.

The fighters had belly tanks and so were in better fuel shape for the flight home. The loose formation rose to 1,000 feet and

how much of your final fuel is available. I landed and, as I hit the deck, felt a huge sigh of relief when that tailhook engaged the wire – taking a deep breath, and giving thanks for my surroundings. They were yelling, "Get out, get out!" I hastened to free the wires, moved up the deck, and managed to get out of the plane, and my crew likewise.

I waited, and I learned later that only one of my five planes had landed beside myself. There were only the two of us I could account for aboard ship. In the next two days, as they were regrouping the pilots and returning them to their respective carriers, I learned that two of my pilots had landed in the water at night ahead of destroyers, and both pilots and crew had been rescued. One plane had landed on another carrier.

Two days later, McLellan and his crew were rescued, having spent two nights in the water in life jackets, separate from each other. They were picked up by patrol boats covering the area.

We were thankful to know that all the torpedo pilots, crews and planes had been accounted for. Six went out and six came back, plus the one who turned back early. It was a miracle when I think of the war. These fellows in McLellan's crew were down, 250 miles from nowhere in open sea, free of anything that might look like land, and alone.

I would never have seen my bombs hit, of course. I relied upon Mac's word. Later, Tom Bronn and his crew reported three more hits. We each carried four 500-pound bombs, armor piercing, delayed action.

I was able to hit the carrier because I was on target as I entered the glide, and I maintained a steady on-target, appropriate lead, I felt. I knew the bombs would fall somewhere near the Japanese carrier, but certainly not on it.

My gunner's name was Jack Webb. He was from Ohio, and we kept track of each other after the war. It was very rare for a torpedo bomber to shoot down a Zero, but he got a Distinguished Flying Cross for that. We recommended him.

I don't know what happened to the pilots who went into the water. Maybe they felt they didn't have enough gas to make one more attempt if they failed. There were all kinds of planes in the landing circle at one time, all out of fuel.

In perfect weather, fighter squadrons would have contests to see how fast they could recover the entire squadron. I think the intervals were up to 60 seconds per plane at maximum. There was no room for error.

That night the intervals were probably longer than that.

After releasing the wire, you'd go straight up the

was on "automatic lean." Sterrie's calm demeanor helped a pilot named LeBlanc. "Hell, if Mr. Sterrie is as cool as all that, why should I fret?"

The night was very dark with no moon and no visible horizon. The planes were traveling very slowly to preserve fuel, and many of the pilots were getting hypnotized by the monotony and drone of the engines. Sterrie was on the edge of falling into a trance, and kept his mind clear by being busy in the cockpit, doing little things.

Sterrie finally picked up the beacon from the U.S. fleet, 60 miles out. Even with his correction to Weymouth's route, he was still too far north. The carriers had been steaming west to close the gap, but now that the planes were returning, the ships turned east to head into the wind.

Mitscher was once again faced with a difficult decision. The returning planes would have trouble finding the carriers in the dark, but to light up the fleet would be to invite an enemy attack. In the end, the admiral decided in favor of the pilots and crews. "Turn on the lights," he ordered. It was 8:52 p.m. The pilots were also told to land on any carrier they could find.

With little fuel and faced with a night landing in crowded conditions, "the pilots' anxiety had turned to desperation."

On the Lexington, only six planes had landed when a rogue SB2C, breaking the landing pattern and cutting in line out of desperation, crashed into a plane that had just landed. Two were killed and five injured in the crash, and 18 minutes after Mitscher had ordered the lights turned on, Lexington turned its lights off to indicate to the pilots that it had a fouled deck.

By 9:20, ten minutes later, the lights were on again.

The pilots reported later that the searchlights, probing the air, and the star shells fired into deck as far as you're directed, wherever they told you. If the people in charge of the deck told you to fold the wings, you'd do so before you got out of the plane. It depended if they were having parking problems on the deck.

Most of the pilots who had landed on the wrong carriers came home the next day. I remember one fighter pilot crashing. He had survived everything that had happened the day previous, the night landing and all, and crashed into the rear of the ship in coming back for his final time. I don't think he survived that crash.

Thus ends the Battle for Saipan.

ON CARRIER LANDINGS

If a pilot just took off, and he had to come back to the

Anti-aircraft gunners aboard the USS Lexington search the sky during the Battle of the Philippine Sea in June 1944. (U.S. Navy photo)

Lt. Cmdr. Ralph Weymouth, who commanded the bombers aboard the Lexington, reports to Admiral Mitscher during the action around Saipan. (U.S. Navy photo)

ship, he couldn't land with a full tank of gas. There was no way to get rid of it. If he was airborne, he could fly around until he got rid of it, or at least part of it. Once, I had suspected engine trouble on the first round. I landed a TBD fully loaded with gas. I released my bombs before I got in the landing circle. But that landing blew out two tires.

The carriers also couldn't launch and recover at the same time, because there would be planes waiting to take off and they would be lined up all the way back. If a plane was in trouble and had to land, you did what you had to do. It depended on how much time you had.

When landing, I don't think I ever aimed for the first wire. That would have been luck in several directions. Lucky you made it, and lucky to catch a wire. Probably two, three or four were the optimum wires to catch.
They would let you know by radio if it's time to come in, like recovering an air patrol or so forth. The torpedo planes were never worried about that. It was

the sky created a dazzling and confusing sky. Sterrie brought his group down to 500 feet to get into a landing pattern, but immediately found the sky too crowded at that altitude and went back up to 1,000 feet.

At that point it was pretty much every pilot for himself as they tried different carriers, attempting to get into landing circles, only to be bumped out at the last second by a "rogue" or "stray" aircraft whose pilot felt he had to bust the pattern in order to land.

At 9:30 p.m., Sterrie landed on the Lexington, and as he was still trying to free his tailhook and move up the deck, he got a radio message from Thomas.

"Hello, Norm," came the calm, matter-of fact-voice. "This is Buzz. I'm going in the water."

Sterrie got the plane out of harm's way, and climbed out. Webb and Klingbiel were already on the deck. "Well, boys, I got you home again," Sterrie said.

In the ready room, the other pilots gathered around Sterrie, clapping him on the back and congratulating him on the mission. Sterrie, however, would have none of the celebrating. He was "haggard and unsmiling,"

time when it was time. The skipper always landed first, and then the order in which you were airborne, or by your formation. Always skipper first, you know that.

A photo in the St. Paul Pioneer Press showed some of the leaders of the Lexington's air group. Sterrie, right, commanded the torpedo bomber group. Weymouth, second from left, commanded the bombers, and Buie, second from right, led the fighters on the carrier. Lt. Cmdr. E.M. Snowden, center, was the overall skipper of the squadron. Lt. Alexander Vraciu, left, shot down six Japanese planes in the Turkey Shoot.

Vice Admiral Marc Mitscher himself signed the citation for Sterrie's third Navy Cross.

Sterrie's entry into his logbook for June 20, 1944, states "Attack on Jap Fleet." He logged it as five hours. It was his 275th carrier landing, and probably his most dramatic.

his thoughts on his fellow pilots Thomas and McLellan. He took a brandy and pineapple juice and settled down to wait.

Ten minutes later, Cushman walked in. Sterrie went over to greet him. "I'm damn glad to see you," he said. Cushman told him that he had landed with only five minutes of fuel left.

The scene in the fleet was pure chaos. One pilot from the Lexington, Cookie Cleland, tried two landings on the Lexington, two landings on the Princeton, one landing on a destroyer, and two more attempts on the Enterprise, where he finally was waved in by the flight control officer. As he taxied up the deck, his engine died – completely out of fuel.

On the Enterprise, two planes landed at exactly the same time. One plane caught the fifth wire and the other caught the second wire. Both were OK. On another carrier, a Japanese torpedo plane, apparently also out of desperation, tried to land. He was waved off and never seen again.

In all that night, Lexington landed 22 planes, including 10 of her own.

In the Mission Beyond Darkness, the Lexington's air group lost nine of its 34 planes, and four of the 64 men who left the flight deck that day.

Chapter Seven
Homecoming

About a week after the closing of the Battle of Saipan, we made sure Guam was not a threat. We made our final attacks on Guam before going home. In doing so, we lost one plane, shot down, and the Navy never recovered the crew. Nobody saw it happen. Nobody knew it happened. It was part of my flight. One dive bomber was also shot down, but he was recovered.

That was all of the war for Air Group 16. That was the last of our strikes. They kept us out of action while the whole fleet went back to Majuro to refurbish and get ready for the next operations. The air crews flew to Wake and went home by ship. We ultimately got back to San Francisco after leave.

I got assigned to Fleet Air Alameda. I was the assistant to the former group commander Ernie Snowden. He was a native of Milford, South Carolina. I covered the office while Snowden slept off a drunk – almost every day. He was a great pilot and commanding officer, but he was an alcoholic.

Did I miss being at sea? Hell, no. It looks glamorous on news reels and all that stuff, but there's a certain amount of repetitive service.

I do have one very fond memory. I used to go up on the deck at the close of the day. I had a portable radio, and sometimes I could catch the skip of the radio signal just right and hear the Mormon Tabernacle Choir from Salt Lake City. It came in beautifully above deck. I'd watch the

When Sterrie got to NAS Alameda, it was his chance to fly several other types of Navy aircraft in addition to the TBF Avenger. Two of those aircraft were the F4U-1D Corsair, above, and the F6F-3 Hellcat, below, both fighter aircraft. Sterrie's logbook also shows he flew the SNJ-5 Texan, a trainer, and the JRB-4 Expediter, a two-engine plane often used by the Coast Guard. Sterrie would fly 10 to 20 times a month at Alameda.

At Naval Air Station Alameda, the runways were dug out of San Francisco Bay at the end of Alameda Island. The air station had its claim to historical fame as the site where Lt. Col. James Doolittle's B-25s were loaded on the USS Hornet prior to the Doolittle Raid, the first U.S. strike against Japan itself in World War II.

sunset.

I'd had very little shore duty up to that time. For us it was just waiting until the war was over, anxiously awaiting those atom bomb strikes. We had a little, flaky group of former fleet people, torpedo bombers, dive bombers. Our responsibility was to check all the area squadrons set to go overseas and make sure they were properly equipped. We mostly flew around, screwing around, keeping busy. If we were at home base at Alameda, we shuffled paper, trying to look busy.

When I wanted to fly, I had a choice of a Hellcat, a Corsair and an Avenger. The fighters were fun. I loved that Corsair. I loved to slow roll it, with that long nose. You kind of rolled around that nose.

Corsairs were supposed to replace the F-6, the Hellcat, the workhorse fighter in the Navy, but they were a little tricky on landing. At slow speed, you didn't have the vertical stabilizer control you wanted.

I never wanted to see how high an Avenger could go, and I never attempted to take it up to high altitude. But I did that in a Corsair once at San Diego. I took it up to 24,000 feet. There's not much control of the plane at that altitude. The ailerons were not as cooperative.

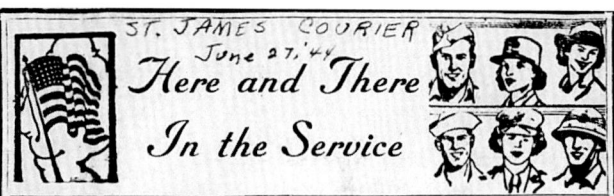

Lt. Norman A. Sterrie Is Vet of 13 Carrier Attacks

Summer Will Mark End of Four Years Active Flying Duty

Branch Naval Public Relations Office — When Lt. Norman A. Sterrie, USNR, goes home to St. James, Minnesota, this summer, he will have completed four years of active flying duty at sea, one of the longest and most useful tours that any naval aviator has put in during this war.

A 26-year-old veteran of thirteen carrier attacks by air groups, Lt. Sterrie continues to refute the popular notion that torpedo bombers lead short lives. It's quite a record, this story of Sterrie, who became Executive Officer of a squadron while still an Ensign, and who otherwise typifies hundreds of fighting Naval Reservists in key positions.

Lugging a tin fish against the Japanese Imperial Navy was a long way from Norman Sterrie's plans when he graduated from Carlton College in 1939, after majoring in pre-medical studies, playing clarinet in the symphony orchestra, and running the quarter-mile and 220 events. But with the foresight that has marked his whole Naval career, he enlisted for flight training in October, 1939, taking his cadet course at Pensacola. Soon Ensign Sterrie was a qualified fleet pilot flying from the Queen of the Flattops, the old Lexington.

The Japs had expected to catch our carriers napping at Pearl Harbor, but it was only a month or so later that those very carriers were raiding the Nips in the Gilberts and Marshalls. By February of 1942 the Lex was cruising around the Solomons with her fighters, led by Jimmy Thach and Butch O'Hare, making the first big bag of Zeroes during the war. On the other side of the ledger were the endless days and weeks

On March 10 came the bold raids on Lae and Salamaua, where Ensign Sterrie and his squadron piloted their obsolete and overloaded torpedo planes in the famous trip over the treacherous Owen Stanley Mountains to destroy many tons of enemy shipping. For his part in this effective strike, Sterrie received his first Navy Cross.

It was in the historic battle of the Coral Seas two months later that Sterrie performed his most colorful work in combat. Not satisfied with a credited torpedo hit on a Jap carrier, Sterrie made a dry run on an enemy cruiser to divert anti-aircraft fire from his squadron commander's plane, which had not yet dropped its tin fish. For this amazing but very successful risk, Sterrie received a second Navy Cross.

Though the big battle was won, the big Lex was lost a few days later, and Ensign Sterrie found himself Executive Officer of a large detachment that grew to 750 men in the course of Odyssean wanderings over the South Seas during the spring of 1942. Upon reaching the States at last, he acquired a charming wife, Betsy, and might have been expected to settle down to a year or so of comfortable shore duty. But by November he had made a lieutenant and become second in command in Bob Isely's torpedo squadron just forming. As one of the very few experienced pilots in the unit "Norman the Foreman" was faced with the nightmares of the early days of the war behind and the difficult job ahead of preparing green pilots for the hardest kind of carrier work. After six months of arduous training, Lt. Sterrie was back in Pacific waters for another crack at the enemy.

This time Lt. Sterrie knew a lot more about carrier strikes, and was able to lead a large number of raids. These included trips to Tarawa, Wake Island (where he won the Air Medal), Mille Atoll, and Kwajalein, where he and his squadron destroyed two Jap cruisers and an ammunition-ship. Such adventures piled up with rapidity. In all these attacks, Sterrie led his division to their targets with cunning and caution, so that no pilot was ever lost in combat, and he hit his individual objectives with excellent results. And with 1944 just getting under way, he is far from through. There will be a few areas of activity that Lt. Sterrie has not seen.

And what as yet unseen area does he want to visit now? Not Truk or Tokyo, but . . . you guessed it . . . a nursery in Minneapolis where Margaret Louise Sterrie, aged five months, is waiting for her capable and long absent father.

Sterrie's hometown newspaper, the St. James Courier, carried this flattering biography in mid-1944.

Homecoming

I remember I worked on getting an instrument rating, although I never used it. The fog would roll in during the evening at Alameda, which was kind of a short field anyway. They dug it out of the bottom of the bay, made an airfield out of it. In order to get out in the morning, you could only do so on instruments. I never did that, but I got an instrument rating in case I would have to some day.

I took a trip down to San Diego and visited with the assignment officer. He told me, "You know, we're getting short on torpedo captains out there." That was that. I would have to go back if they said so, but the war got over. By the book, I never had shore duty. I was always in a squadron.

My wife and my daughter were with me in Alameda. First we lived up in the hills at Oakland in a house that was much too big. It was in Piedmont, or something like that, a suburb of Oakland.

The last page of Sterrie's wartime log book shows his last flight as a combat aviator. He flew a training plane on a four-hour jaunt from NAS Alameda on Sept. 1, 1945, just days after the war ended. The flight brought his total Navy flight hours to 1,623.7. He had 279 carrier landings.

To find a place in Alameda, my wife had to go to work in some defense job. The job lasted about three days before she quit. In that time we managed to rent a place. It was interesting. With all the war I'd experienced, I couldn't find a place to rent. It was all rent-only to war workers. That's the way it was.

We had an apartment then in Alameda. I had to go through a tunnel to get to the air base. I used to watch the Pan-Am clippers anchor out in the bay there. They were a beautiful plane. They flew from Hawaii and other places.

When the war ended, it was first in, first out. I went home three days after Japan surrendered. I had them put together two cruise boxes, big wooden boxes, to send everything home. I still had those two cruise boxes for many years afterward.

I had to get a place to live, and we managed to get a war-built house out near the Minneapolis VA Hospital. The address was 5337 43rd Ave. South.

Like that address, some things stick, like 6-9155, the number I had to call at Pearl Harbor to contact this family that had adopted me during the war years.

The family's name was Ericson, and he was an engineer. We met at a restaurant in downtown Honolulu. It was a very crowded restaurant, and my friend and I had a table. These folks were standing around, and I invited them to come and join us so they could have a place to sit down to eat. It was one of the finest things that ever happened. They had a home up in the valley, the road between Pearl and Kaneohe. They gave me a bedroom and a place to live whenever the ship was in. Plus, I had the privileges at his golf course. So every time the ship came in, I had a way of getting booze, and that was part of a very nice relationship we had during the war and after the war. He had worked for one of the early five corporations that settled Hawaii.

As the war went on, of course, these visits diminished. The times we could get back to Pearl were very limited, and once Majuro was developed as a major fleet landing, it was unthinkable to go all the way back to Pearl Harbor. I saw him after the war; 1954 I think was the last I saw of him. It was pretty nice for me, and I think they enjoyed hearing the tales I was able to tell.

We had thought about Berkeley Medical School, but then we figured it was too far from home. I called the University of Minnesota Medical School. I just assumed you signed up for medicine and they'd take you – like signing up for English 101. I just assumed I'd be admitted, and it worked out that way.

I took some general courses at the University of Minnesota. I was just seeing if I could study again and put my noodle to work. I know one of the courses was about child care. I remember sitting in the office with Medical School Dean Harold Diehl. He advised me to take fun courses, because once you get into medical school, there would be nothing but medicine. I was in the class of 1949. For years we didn't know what class we were in because we were waiting for the rotation to come around, changing from year-round to nine months of university.

When I left Carleton seven years earlier, my roommate and several of my closest friends had gone to medical school. That was sort of a connection I valued. The last year of the war, I was thinking

HOMECOMING

about it. The GI Bill made it possible, of course – and the Navy Reserve. I was still flying one weekend a month.

I had a squadron at Wold-Chamberlain. Ultimately, it was an air group. I know we had at least 12 torpedo planes. We flew with live bombs once out of Bemidji. The idea was to drop them and make big holes for the moose to bathe in. It was north of Twin Lakes up there. I don't know if it worked, but we dropped the bombs. I'm glad I didn't have to put that mission together.

This Sterrie family photo at Carleton College in the fall of 1945 was probably taken after Norm and Don had come home from the war. From left are Norman, Elle, Ole, Eloise and Don. Eloise was a freshman at Carleton that year, following in her brother's footsteps. Peter, an Army pilot in Europe, was not home for this photograph.

Chapter Eight
Music and Medicine

I had lost my clarinet when the ship went down, but my mother-in-law found a good one once we moved back to Minneapolis. I didn't miss it very much at the time, but when I went back to it, I became quite intense with it.

I took lessons on the clarinet for the first time after the war. I had a very good teacher, very demanding. I remember one session we had, and he kind of blew up at me. I said, "Bob, I'm not doing this to be first chair in the philharmonic. This is supposed to be fun for me." He got the message. Lay off.

I had about four years of lessons with him. He was a very good player himself. He had played with the Winnipeg Symphony and the Duluth Symphony.

One thing led to another, and I thought I needed a new clarinet. Coincidentally, Arnie Anderson's son had a music store on 50th and France and the store was having a going-out-of-business sale. Arnie informed me that they had seven Buffet clarinets that were going fast. I put my money down and got a new Buffet, which is what symphony players use mostly.

I think it was a $750 instrument when I bought it, and I used it until just a year or two ago when I got a new one. Now they're a bargain at $1,750. I still have the original one.

Andrea Lubov was a music-based friend of Sterrie's.

We met at a music workshop in the Twin Cities. He was so pleasant to be around, everybody loved to be with Norm. He played mostly clarinet in those days, and he was really quite good. He had a whole lot of skill, plus he was such a pleasant guy to play music with. Music was such a huge part of his life.

I did a couple of trips with Norm. We drove out together to a music workshop in Bozeman, Montana, at Montana State University. We had known each other for a while, but this was the first time he told me anything about his World War II experiences. He told me, "This is the anniversary of the best-worst day of my life." I think it was the day the Lexington was sunk.

That was his last trip to Bozeman, where he had gone many times. He'd had a cornea transplant, and he just couldn't read the music as quickly as he wanted. Later on he had some hearing loss, and then the stroke, and that was the end of the music part of his life.

After Betsy died, a day or two later after the funeral, he asked a friend of his and me to come over and play together. It's not something I could have done, but it was where he wanted to be emotionally.

I also got attracted to chamber music playing after a session out in Bozeman, Montana, where the state university is located. I signed up for that place for a week, not knowing whether I could play well enough not to be a drag on the other people. I went out there all alone, with no support.

I remember the first session. It was a dismal group. And I forgot to use the A clarinet, and tried to play the music with a B-flat, so I was part of the dismal group.

I returned to that place for several summers and enjoyed the chamber playing very much. They had a tremendous library of music that they acquired through the years.

Further explorations into chamber playing happened at the elderhostel at the state university in Colorado. It was at Pingree Park, the summer campus. This elderhostel was the prime one in the United States and had the highest record of returnees that an elderhostel had ever seen. I did this for about 15 years, enjoying the trip out. Some years I would add on a trip to the elderhostel at Hot Springs, Arkansas.

Locally, I played with the Minneapolis Police Band for a number of years, but then quit when we were playing the same numbers over and over and over. It was very tiring.

The Minneapolis Police Band is the oldest continuously playing police band in the United States. It's been around since the time of my birth.

Later, at one of the Lake Harriet concerts, they said, "Come on back, we need you." I rejoined, and stayed with the band until 2007, when I had a stroke, making my right hand useless, and destroying all the music I had done. No more could I play the clarinet as I used to.

I also played oboe in the Health Sciences Orchestra at the University of Minnesota for a while. I always found time. It seems that if you have a priority, it doesn't interfere with work at all. Rehearsals were always at night anyway.

Sterrie traveled around the country participating in music groups.

I played the English horn in the Police Band for a few years, and then went to the bassoon. All of these were self-taught. Finally the bassoon got too heavy to carry, and I had to give that up.

You never knew in advance what you would be assigned in these chamber places. I remember one instructor who was so demanding that we did it one measure at a time. We sat for two full hours, and in that time we accomplished about four measures. One of the players left crying. I wanted to tell the fellow to knock it off and give us some real teaching. He never returned. I think he was asked not to return again.

I'm always threatening to go back to the guitar, now that I can't play the clarinet. But now I'm finding that pretty difficult. I think I could strum, but my left hand is now touched with this stroke. I try now and then to play the clarinet, but I can't cover the holes adequately, and the air leaks out and there goes the note.

As a member of the Minneapolis Police Band.

I love to listen to the Minnesota Orchestra. They're on public radio on Friday nights. I have quite a library of music I've accumulated through the years.

We gave piano lessons to Margaret, and she became the accompanist to the Southwest High School Choral Group. Later on, she applied and was accepted at Stanford University. She studied French and foreign service. She later went into the Peace Corps and taught in Kenya, Africa.

We adopted a son, George, at 19 months. He has developed into a very nice young man. He has been trained in a number of fields, and is now a welder. Unfortunately, he recently developed colon cancer, and was operated on and is in a state of recovery right now.

My wife died in 1998, and I have been single since.

Sterrie practiced almost every day until a stroke took away his music at age 90.

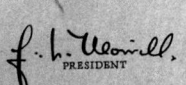

Sterrie's medical degree from the University of Minnesota.

BACK HOME

I had made the decision to go into pediatrics back when I was at Carleton. One reason was that pediatrics was one year shorter in its residency program. It was a two-year program at the time, and internal medicine was three years. I didn't know how I'd stretch the funds that far. The major choices were internal medicine, pediatrics and obstetrics. Surgery was a little out of the question because it took extra time.

At the university, the head of the hospitals called the whole class together one time, and said he was perplexed because not one person in our class had made an intention to take any specialties at the University of Minnesota. They were all going someplace else. He was mystified. And, of course, we let him have it about their teaching.

That must have changed, because they did wind up with several in obstetrics and even surgery. The doctors there had been very brutal to us, not very kind. The war had just been over, and there were not only medical students, but residencies, people coming back to finish what they had started before the war. It was a problem for various departments, and certainly a hurdle they had to contend with. Medical students were pretty low on the pole of course.

Dr. Lawrence Vorlicky *worked with Sterrie at the Park-Nicollet Clinic, and he was a good friend and hunting and fishing companion through the years. He left the clinic in 1986 to take a teaching position at Dartmouth University.*

I joined the clinic in 1966, and Norm had been there already a long time. He wasn't a founder, but he came shortly thereafter. There was a close-knit, struggling group of pediatricians at that time, and we all became friends and did hunting and fishing together.

Three of us leased some hunting property on Grove Lake, and we found out pretty quick that there were damn few ducks. On opening day, we'd spend about 20 minutes trying to shoot the Grove Lake duck, but then Norm and I would go into a little slough and spend the rest of the day catching frogs. Then later we'd have martinis and frog legs. That was our opening day.

Norm was on the board of trustees at the clinic, and later he became president of the clinic. He was responsible for the development of the new clinic. Norm was quietly a very strong person. People appreciated him because he did a good job. He was never flaky. He was the rock of Gibraltar. What Norm said you could take to the bank.

In the field of pediatric allergy, he was well regarded. He had his own department within the clinic

By department or individual, you were exposed to attitudes. Some of the clerks or some of the people on top were not always thoughtful. I remember one student, following behind a professor, actually tripped the fellow, hoping he'd fall and kill himself, I suppose. That was a reputation some of the people had.

Medical school had come pretty easily for me. I loved to study. The trouble was when examinations came, they were not always in agreement with my personal life. I was still flying for the Navy one weekend a month, and if that fell during an exam period, then that's the way it was.

I think child care had great appeal for me. This only became fortified during my internship. I had a general internship at Minneapolis General Hospital, going through all phases of medicine. It took a year, a month here and a month there. It was a full rotation with 12 different areas, starting out with wherever you happened to fall into the 12. God help those who had to be with the ambulance interns the first month. They didn't have any experience.

During that time I had two sleepless months, obstetrics and orthopedics. In those days, there was no regard for your sleep. If the work demanded it, you

Betsy and Norm in the 1980s.

At age 62, Sterrie prepared his Honda Gold Wing for a trip to Wisconsin with his buddies.

Betsy and Norm in 1996.

for pediatric allergy. At that time, there were no specialists outside of downtown Minneapolis, and Norm was competing with these old guys. They thought we were carpet baggers, or socialists or communists. There was a lot of negative feeling.

But the St. Louis Park Clinic, as it was called, was a first-rate clinic from the get-go.

We all knew he was a Navy flier, but we knew little about what he had done. I don't think anybody knew he had won three Navy Crosses. We knew that one of the flattops he was on had been sunk. But that was fairly typical of World War II vets. They didn't talk about their service a lot.

There was nothing flamboyant about Norman. He was droll. He always saw the interesting part of something. I won't say he was cynical, but he saw the satiric side of things. He was just a good guy. He had a strong center. He was honest and trustworthy.

went 24 hours day. Usually you shared the month with two others, taking calls and so forth, dividing it up.

I remember the period in the eye phase. A fellow showed up at the eye clinic and wanted to get some glasses in a hurry because he wanted to go deer hunting the next week, and he couldn't see 10 feet. That's how important deer hunting was to him. The glasses, though, were probably more important to his fellow hunters than they were to him.

I did two more years in the residency, and then it was time to find a job. It wasn't difficult to find job openings. My wife and I took a trip from Crookston to Grand Forks to Great Falls, Montana. There were all these openings. There was a need in these areas. Ultimately, we came to Worthington.

PRACTICING

I had considered becoming a general practitioner. There was no GP program at that time – that came later. My orientation, growing up in the small town, was knowing the small-town doctors and how they worked. That appealed to me very much.

I wanted to go to a small community. Actually, that's why I went to Worthington for my first year of practice. Plus I wanted to be near my parents, who were becoming elderly.

Also, I had wanted to practice in a clinic situation, and there were some very fine clinics in those days. I did not want to practice alone. In a clinic situation, you have all the backup, including the time off and vacation planning and that sort of thing. If you're alone, you're stuck with it.

Betsy never worked after I started medical school. She could have, but we had the youngster. She became part of the neighborhood, and we felt very at home in the neighborhood. We lived on Smith Avenue in Worthington. We owned a nice house on a well-developed street just two blocks from the clinic. I could get home at noon. I started practicing piano at the time, so I would grab a quick sandwich and sit down at the piano on a daily basis. That was my fondest remembrance of Worthington — plus all the fine fellows I worked with. We were there a year.

My next stop was at St. Louis Park Medical Center, which later became Park-Nicollet. I joined the original associates who had wanted me to come there in the first place. They had known me in residency. They were my fellow travelers.

There were 11 of them. The surgeon had gotten together with 10 others to form this clinic. It was at the junction of what is now Highway 100 and Excelsior Boulevard. He took a count of what the traffic was there. I think it was 35,000 cars a day, even at that time. He said, "That's where we ought to be."

Of course the area was mostly gravel roads at that time. Highway 100 was a pretty dangerous route. No mid line, just a path.

I was probably the 12th or 14th doctor to join the clinic. I was an early recruit. I was the third pediatrician to join, and we were very busy. It was a developing area. We'd head out to the little row houses -- house calls all the time. When they were trying to convince me to come to the clinic, the two other pediatricians, George Lund and Arnie Anderson, invited me to dinner at the Andersons' house. The two of them were so damn busy, they never got to dinner. And they were recruiting me.

It was what I expected. Plenty of backup, house calls every night. But the growth of the clinic depended on us. There were many kids around that needed help. There were all the house calls at night, but I don't think I ever got tired of it. Mostly you got to know the parents. I suppose there was a mutual need for each other.

I built a house on 43rd and Abbott in the far west of Minneapolis. I built a split level for $22,000, and Arnie Anderson, the head of the clinic, said, "If you did all that for $22,000, you're our new building boss." I was in charge of all building probably for the next 20 years.

From the Park-Nicollet Clinic Bulletin, January 2005.
Dr. Arnold Anderson, *a co-founder of the clinic, wrote the following excerpt as part of a history and memoir of the clinic.*

When Norman Sterrie, MD, joined St. Louis Park Medical Center in 1953, he pioneered pediatric allergy as a subspecialty. There were no training sites in Minnesota, so Dr. Sterrie created his own curriculum by studying immunology at the laboratory of Robert Good, MD, at the University of Minnesota and clinical allergy with an adult allergist in the private sector (who also taught at the University). Dr. Sterrie also created and directed the weekly pediatric clinic at the University and later at Hennepin County General Hospital.
All the while, his pediatric allergy practice at the St. Louis Park Medical Center site was continuing to grow.

There were arguments about expansion, of course. We lost one doctor, I know, who was unwilling to go through one more expansion. But we made an early decision that we would expand according to need, and that has held ever since – from the early 11 doctors to the present over 600. Plus, there were the buildings such as the hospital and huge clinics.

I was president of the clinic from 1970 to 1975, and at that time we had about 80 doctors. It was a time of emerging computer technology, in the business world at least. We were transforming our business, and making that transition into computer mode was almost painful. We had offers of management help from IBM and a St. Paul firm. We opted for the St. Paul firm because they had been so helpful along the way.

Sterrie had a series of hunting dogs over the years that he loved dearly.

Eloise, Peter, Don and Norm at a family gathering.

During the term I was president I found it very difficult to discharge physicians. Their whole life had been spent in education up to that point. But some never found or never mixed into our needs. I think this happened in five instances, but it was always the board that made the decision. It wasn't my lone decision, so I had that backup, anyway, in difficult times.

I did not really ask for the president's job, but they needed help and I was put up because of my long experience with the building program and my overall knowledge of the clinic and how it operated.

The trials of having a group of specialists accept family practitioners as equals was a battle in itself. We developed a program for generalists. There was some pretty stiff opposition, but ultimately they saw things my way. If we were going to continue to grow, it wouldn't be through specialists. The bulk of need was for family physicians, but developing a situation where we had enough family physicians was a problem in itself. There weren't any around, so we started to train our own. The University of Minnesota spotted this and agreed to come over on its own terms, which were not very good. They had the gall to agree to move into our space and do all the management, take all the funds, and we would have to pay the people to support the program. This was not acceptable. I said, "Get the hell out of here."

Sterrie when he was president of the Park-Nicollet Clinic.

Sterrie about two weeks before he died in 2008.

I think eventually, to bolster family practitioners, the university developed a program, it got state funds of $400,000 to do this, and after that time there became a source of family practitioners.

Developing our own program was not an easy one. It was very difficult to resolve differences that these fellows could not resolve themselves on who was in charge, who should get this time off and who should get that time off and so forth. That's a good picture of early practice in Minnesota.

Personally, I never trusted the system. One of the early ones ahead of me was thrown out, voted out, because he saw the need for central billing. When I became head, I couldn't see it any other way. Everybody was billing differently, and it made no sense. It was not fair to everybody, and it was not understandable – to management at least. Having observed that other doctor lose his position, how could I trust the system? We were fortunate in having a wonderful all-clinic manager, highly respected and with a good head on his shoulders.

I always felt I had 70 vice presidents all giving information at the same time on how to run the place.

The lack of a plan at the time meant that the last person to survive got the whole ball of wax. That was not acceptable either. We finally decided to be a non-profit association of doctors. And it had to be a plan acceptable to the Internal Revenue Service, which we accomplished.

In the early years, we sent our allergy patients downtown, but we found out that we were being bad-mouthed by the people we were referring to. That would not do. They said, "Norman, you have all the allergies, so you're our next allergist." It takes one to know one.

I took up allergy and had the clinic at Hennepin General Hospital for 10 years. That was my training ground. After that I took the boards, and I could call myself an allergist. In a limited way in the changeover, I did both pediatrics and allergy, but

Someone convinced Sterrie to try on his flight gear and pose outside his house on Lake Harriet.

when our fifth allergist came, we decided we were going to be an allergy department, and that's what we became. We had pediatric allergists and internal medicine allergists.

I had asthma as a child, and I had an interest in asthma. We never cured anything in allergies, but through the years the drugs have been so improved, and the appearance of steroids on the market has changed the whole program on allergies. Treatment programs have been devised and publicized so that anybody developing asthma now has a protocol of treatment. Every year a lecture is given by a leading allergist in the country, and it's named after me. Invitations are sent out to all of the allergists in town. It was a way to have them meet each other. It could help them resolve any differences they might have among themselves.

I retired as an allergist. Now, I'm not connected to the clinic in any way – except as a patient.

Music and Medicine